We would like to recognize and th.
Their support provides the Americ
of New Jersey with the ability to 〈
and prepare for our i

GUARDIAN
$10,000 +

≈

ADVOCATE
$3,000 - $9,999

Hopkins, Sampson & Brown Real Estate Advisory Services, LLC
McCarter & English, LLP
McCusker, Anselmi, Rosen & Carvelli, PC

≈

AMICUS
$1,500 - $2,999

Margee & Douglas Greenberg
Pashman Stein, PC
Porzio Governmental Affairs
Hazel S. Stix & Harold Borkan
The William H. Buckman Law Firm

On the Frontlines of Freedom

A CHRONICLE OF THE FIRST 50 YEARS OF THE AMERICAN CIVIL LIBERTIES UNION OF NEW JERSEY

MARY JO PATTERSON

AMERICAN CIVIL LIBERTIES UNION OF NEW JERSEY

On the Frontlines of Freedom
A Chronicle of the First 50 Years of the American Civil Liberties Union of New Jersey

iUniverse books may be ordered through booksellers or by contacting:

American Civil Liberties Union of New Jersey
P.O. Box 32159
Newark, NJ 07102

ISBN: 978-1-4697-6091-9 (sc)
ISBN: 978-1-4697-6377-4 (hc)
ISBN: 978-1-4697-6092-6 (ebk)

Printed in the United States of America
iUniverse rev. date: 03/12/2012

This book is dedicated to the thousands who have helped the American Civil Liberties Union of New Jersey bring progress to people's doorsteps by courageously standing up for our rights.

ACKNOWLEDGMENTS

When the ACLU of New Jersey embarked on this book project in 2010, we began by asking former clients, staffers, cooperating attorneys and volunteers to dig deep into their attics and their memories for stories, photos, documents and details about their time with the ACLU-NJ. And they did, offering generous amounts of time and material so we could weave together the colorful history of the ACLU of New Jersey.

We are grateful to the many clients interviewed in this book who were willing to spend hours reliving sometimes painful memories about their legal battles and the circumstances leading up to the moment they decided to take a stand for their rights.

We thank Angel Dominguez, Deborah Ellis, Sally Frank, Bernard Freamon, Frank Askin, Lenora Lapidus, Steve Latimer, Jane Lifset, Lawrence Lustberg, Leora Mosston, Stephen Nagler, Bruce Rosen, William Buckman, Benjamin S. Laves, Neil Mullin, Ed Martone, Edith Oxfeld, Henry di Suvero, Howard Levine, Michael Berger, Lennox Hinds, Jeff Fogel, Robert Curvin and Herbert Waldman among many others. We wish to thank the tireless researchers at the Newark Public Library, the Willingboro Public Library, The New Jersey Historical Society, The Star-Ledger, Rutgers School of Law-Newark and The New Jersey Law Journal who dug through their archives to fish out historic photographs.

We are also grateful to ACLU-NJ board member Peggy Brooks for her sharp eye and editing skills and to the ACLU-NJ staff members who contributed with their feedback.

Finally we wish to thank Mary Jo Patterson, whose dogged reporting unearthed triumphant stories that will undoubtedly inspire the next generation of civil libertarians.

Katie Wang
ACLU-NJ Communications Director
MARCH 2012

TABLE OF CONTENTS

INTRODUCTION *1*

CHAPTER 1

THE BIRTH OF AN ORGANIZATION *5*
A Soldier Fights to Buy a Home

CHAPTER 2

SOCIAL UPHEAVAL *23*
A Brawl Divides an Emotionally Raw City

CHAPTER 3

KNOCKING DOWN BARRIERS *41*
A Widower Takes on the Social Security Administration

CHAPTER 4

ASSAULTS ON THE BILL OF RIGHTS............... *63*
One Teacher Risks His Career

CHAPTER 5

UNEASE IN THE AGE OF PROSPERITY *81*
Peace Activists Stake New Ground for Free Speech

CHAPTER 6

ATTACK ON AMERICAN SOIL....................... *99*
Fresh Threats to Civil Liberties

AFTERWORD *121*

This book examines the first 50 years of the American Civil Liberties Union of New Jersey. The ACLU-NJ was founded in 1960 in Newark as an offshoot of the much older American Civil Liberties Union, a national nonpartisan organization based in New York. Like its parent, the New Jersey affiliate was established to defend the freedoms guaranteed all individuals under the U.S. Constitution. But it had its own personality, full of fighting spirit and willing to take on anyone, or any governmental body, infringing on personal liberties.

In the summer of 1960, when the ACLU-NJ came into being, New Jersey may have looked like a placid place. Yet under the surface the organization's founders perceived currents of injustice. They were disturbed that so much of the state was racially segregated, and that housing discrimination was overt and widespread. They were troubled that young people were being swept into the juvenile justice system without any of the rights afforded adults charged with violations of law. They were concerned that compulsory Bible reading in the public schools breached the wall separating church and state. And they began working to address those issues, in communities, in the state Legislature and in the courts.

Most of these issues were not new. Some of the founders had been involved in civil liberties causes for years, on their own or through local committees associated with the national ACLU. New Jersey's courts had been thrust into a number of notorious First Amendment fights, including the battle between Jersey City Mayor Frank "I am the Law" Hague and labor unions. (The U.S. Supreme Court decided the case in 1939, ruling against Boss Hague and in favor of the Committee for Industrial Organization.) New Jersey had also experienced its share of civil liberties battles in the late 1940s and 1950s, when fear of Communist subversion prompted governments and institutions to demand loyalty oaths from citizens.

The ACLU-NJ's earliest causes may seem tame. One of its first skirmishes with government came a few months after its founding. Late one night in February of 1961, East Orange police raided the homes of 16 residents — some of whom had already gone to bed — and arrested them for ignoring summonses to return overdue library books. Three library patrons, unable to post bail, spent the night in jail. The ACLU-NJ compared the police to "the Gestapo" and kicked up such a fuss that future raids were cancelled. The ACLU-NJ also embarked on a spirited attack on censorship. Four county prosecutors had banned Henry Miller's "Tropic of Cancer," Camden arrested a bookseller, and Montclair was considering a proposal for a film censorship commission.

Other urgent issues arose soon enough. By 1964 civil rights unrest began rocking New Jersey's cities. Major disorders exploded in 1967 in Newark and Plainfield, and the ACLU-NJ turned its attention to police brutality and racial discrimination. Then opposition to the Vietnam War pulled it into draft counseling and litigation against the Selective Service System. During the 1970s the civil rights movement broadened, and the ACLU-NJ launched special projects to help other groups, including women, prisoners and farmworkers. The 1980s produced sustained campaigns on behalf of gay rights, and against racial profiling; the 1990s required new fights for established rights, such as abortion. After 9/11, the ACLU-NJ veered in yet another direction, challenging national security policy and defending non-citizens under investigation for possible links to terrorism.

Some of the people who turned to the ACLU-NJ made front-page news. There was Stephen Wiesenfeld, the single father who sued the Social Security Administration for denying him a surviving spouse benefit after his wife died in childbirth. There was Sally Frank, the Princeton University student who spent more than a decade battling Princeton's male-only eating clubs. And there was Jeff May, the teacher who risked his career to challenge a state law that required public schools to start the day with a moment of silence. Most, though, were people with names few would recall — the senior class president barred from graduation because his sideburns did not conform to the school district's dress code; the county college professors threatened with defamation for criticizing the chairman of their college's board of trustees; the truck driver given a ticket by a state trooper for not speaking English; and the high school student who was told she couldn't wear a red "life" armband to participate in a day of solidarity against abortion.

Not all represented popular causes. The ACLU-NJ defends free speech regardless of message. At times, clients have included groups like the Ku Klux Klan and neo-Nazis. "We believe the Klan, like any other group, should be able to express its opinion, no matter how despicable we think that opinion is," legal director Deborah Ellis explained in 1990, after defending the Klan's right to march in Millville. The ACLU-NJ once charged state and local police with harassing three alleged mobsters by writing them up for hundreds of phony motor vehicle violations. It defended a train conductor who was fired for burning the Quran at a protest against an Islamic center in Manhattan on his day off. It represented individuals peacefully protesting the homes of physicians providing legal abortion services.

The organization takes a stand on government policy affecting individual rights — and sticks to it — whether it's the death penalty, public school funding, or privacy in Internet communications. Much of its work is done out of sight. It educates. It sends letters. It negotiates, seeking to resolve issues without a legal fight. When it does go to court, it may not always win, but it will have taken a stand and elevated public awareness of an issue. It does not charge clients.

These days, the organization looks a lot different from the way it looked in 1960. Back then it had neither office nor staff. Today the ACLU-NJ, still in Newark, has 14 staffers and 15,000 members who support its work. But its mission hasn't changed a bit.

Mary Jo Patterson

CHAPTER ONE

The Birth of an Organization

A Soldier Fights to Buy a Home

Prospective buyers line up to tour a model home on the opening day at Levittown, N.J., on June 7, 1958.
(Willingboro Public Library)

The furor started in the summer of 1958, when a reporter asked builder William Levitt if he planned to sell to blacks in his newest housing development in Willingboro, N.J., a farm community midway between Trenton and Camden. Levitt, plainly and unapologetically, said "no."

The developer had established a whites-only policy in older Levitt communities in Levittown, N.Y., and Levittown, Pa., and saw no reason to do anything differently now. "If we sell one house to a Negro family, then 90 to 95 percent of our white customers will not buy into the community. That is their attitude, not ours. We did not create it, and we cannot cure it," he told the Saturday Evening Post. "We can solve a housing problem or we can try to solve a racial problem, but we cannot combine the two."

Levitt was soon forced to eat his words. America was changing, and he had missed the signs. Willie R. James, an African-American barred from buying in Willingboro, filed discrimination charges that summer against the mighty Levitt & Sons Inc. James' lawyer, Emerson Darnell, a mild-mannered Quaker from Mount Holly and future founding board member of the American Civil Liberties Union of New Jersey, argued the whites-only policy was discriminatory and illegal. The New Jersey Supreme Court agreed with Darnell, and integration came to Willingboro.

Bill Levitt revolutionized homebuilding by mass-producing thousands of homes for the post-World War II generation. He was a superb salesman, marketing an affordable version of the American Dream. But he underestimated the power of the budding civil rights movement. He failed to envision the chilly reception awaiting him in New Jersey. And he did not foresee the determination of Willie James, a 38-year-old man who — like hundreds of others lined up outside the model homes off Route 130 that June of 1958 — saw his family's future unfolding inside a Levitt home.

When a sales agent refused to sell to him, "I was shocked. He was so bold about it. He said, 'We don't sell homes to blacks,' " James told an interviewer nearly 40 years later. By then the father of seven, long since retired from the Army and retired from a second career as an equal opportunity officer with ITT Corporation, was a civil rights leader and ordained minister. It was a story he would tell many times.

James was born in Vidalia, La., in 1920 and grew up in the South during the Jim Crow era. During his childhood an uncle was lynched by a white mob, according to Jerome Johnson, a friend in Willingboro. James attended Southern University in Baton Rouge, and was drafted in 1941. He was stationed in Fort Dix from 1946

until 1951, three years after President Harry S. Truman ordered
the Army desegregated. Then he was transferred to Europe. While
there James lodged a complaint against a German restaurant that
refused to serve him, according to a short biography published
by the Willingboro branch of the National Association for the
Advancement of Colored People. The restaurant was located in
the French zone of occupied Germany, and a French judge ordered
the restaurant closed. In 1955 James returned to Fort Dix. One
day he read that Levitt planned to build 16,000 homes in nearby
Willingboro, and decided to fill out an application.

Willingboro had only 150 or so houses, but Levitt had bought
up about 90 percent of the township's vacant land and planned
to construct 15,000 housing units on it. His master plan called
for a community of winding roads branching off from a broad
landscaped parkway, complete with sewage and water systems,
schools, and stores. Levittown, N.Y., and Levittown, Pa., had
proved popular with blue-collar workers, but he aimed the New
Jersey development at the middle class. Homes were designed
with young children in mind; they came in three styles starting at
$11,490, with a down payment of $350. Every home had the latest
General Electric appliances, and every neighborhood had its own
school and swimming pool. Willingboro politicians approved
the plan, no doubt happy Levitt was donating the schools, and
held a referendum changing the town's name from Willingboro
to Levittown. (The referendum passed in 1959, but the name
reverted to Willingboro in a second referendum in 1963.)

Levitt dropped his racial bomb at a press conference in
Washington, D.C., on June 5, 1958. It was not surprising that a
reporter asked about race. The previous summer, Daisy and Bill
Meyers, a black couple who bought a resale home in Levittown,
Pa., had been greeted by taunts and rock-throwing neighbors.
What's more, New Jersey had just amended its civil rights law to
ban discrimination in housing assisted by federal subsidies — and
Levitt depended heavily on mortgage insurance from the Federal
Housing Administration.

Levitt's insistence on white-only homebuyers drew immediate fire. The American Civil Liberties Union, NAACP, Knights of Columbus, and American Jewish Committee formed a New Jersey Committee Against Discrimination in Housing. State officials complained to the FHA. Patrick Murphy Malin, executive director of the ACLU, dashed off a letter to the New Jersey attorney general asking him to revoke the company's corporation charter. "Mr. Levitt is not only promoting bigotry," Malin wrote. "He is proposing to create a township dedicated to the principle of segregation."

Willie James, apparently unbowed by the fuss, went to the model home sales office. When a salesman turned him away, he conferred with a friend employed by the state Division Against Discrimination. A few days later, James filed a complaint with the division.

Levitt launched a fierce legal offensive. First he tried to prevent the division from investigating. When a state court ordered the division to proceed, he attacked its jurisdiction in the matter. But Emerson Darnell, the American Civil Liberties Union lawyer, maintained Levitt's whites-only sales policy violated the Bill of Rights provision of the New Jersey State Constitution, enacted in 1947, and the housing amendment to the New Jersey Law Against Discrimination, passed in 1957. Levitt lost every step of the way, but kept on building. By the time *Levitt & Sons Inc. v. Division Against Discrimination* reached the New Jersey Supreme Court, he had sold 2,000 homes. Levitt made a last-ditch appeal to the U.S. Supreme Court, which eventually refused to hear the case. In their successful motion to have the case dismissed, Darnell and the other attorneys involved referred to Levitt's fight as an attempt to "twist a state ban of racial discrimination into an impediment to federal policy."

In the meantime, Levitt announced a "voluntary" integration program. "Sooner or later the present New Jersey law, or some other law substantially like it, will be upheld and enforced no matter how the present litigation turns out, and sooner or later some Negro families will move into Levittown," he said. His company formed a Council on Human Relations to prepare for that

Emerson Darnell

Emerson Darnell had just passed the state bar exam when a partner in a large Camden law firm invited him to lunch. He offered Darnell a job as an associate in the firm. When it became clear, however, that Darnell would have to discontinue his pro bono work with the ACLU, he did not hesitate to decline the offer.

Born and raised in Medford, Darnell was a conscientious objector during World War II and started doing pro bono work with the ACLU after he finished law school. He founded the South Jersey chapter of the Philadelphia ACLU and went on to become a founder of the ACLU-NJ. He served on the board of directors for 39 years.

As a volunteer attorney for the ACLU-NJ, Darnell defended the rights of the Ku Klux Klan (which had sought to march in Millville), anti-war activists, Hispanic motorists targeted by race on the New Jersey Turnpike, and gay men entrapped in public restrooms by undercover police. He was also a lead attorney in the case that brought about the integration of Willingboro Township after developers Levitt & Sons Inc. refused to sell homes to African Americans.

In 1992 Darnell was the recipient of the ACLU-NJ's Roger N. Baldwin Civil Liberties Award, "for his gallant struggle to vindicate the constitutional rights of all persons however unpopular." Looking back on his career, Darnell said, "To me the challenge of practicing law has been how to make things 'fairer,' in my own small way."

prospect, and hired Harold Lett, an African-American recently retired from the state's civil rights division, to run it. Lett enlisted local ministers and civic leaders in the pro-integration campaign. On June 27, 1958, Levitt, capitulating to integration, announced that "Two Negro families are in the process of buying homes in (Levittown). In view of the expressed wish of both these families to be spared notoriety, no further details about them will be made public at this time." One of those families, of course, was the family of Willie R. James. Civil rights groups urged James to move in on a weekday, when fewer people were likely to be home. He chose a Saturday. "I was not going to sneak around," said James, who became president of the Burlington County and Willingboro chapters of the NAACP. "Either people were going to accept us, or they weren't." By and large, they did. On the family's first day at 32 Marchmont Lane, James came home to find a white neighbor helping his wife hang curtains.

Herbert J. Gans, a sociologist studying the evolution of the new town, praised the Levitt team for defusing white hostility in his 1967 book "The Levittowners." In each new subdivision, salesmen offered black families first dibs on the most desirable streets, typically those bordering woods or creeks. The salesmen also made sure they did not sell adjoining homes to blacks. Relatively few black families moved in, however; by 1964, there were only about 50.

Even Emerson Darnell, James' lawyer, cut Levitt some slack, according to his son, Chris Darnell. "My father said Levitt was not necessarily a racist and was primarily a businessman. When it became clear that this was a mistake and the community was against it, Levitt really became an advocate for integration and was not an obstacle," he said.

The Levittown case became a rallying point for civil libertarians at opposite ends of New Jersey to unite under one roof. In the north was Emil Oxfeld, a labor lawyer with a long history of volunteering for the ACLU. In the south was Emerson Darnell, affiliated with the Greater Philadelphia ACLU. A statewide New Jersey ACLU affiliate had been under discussion for years. In a press release dated June 1, 1960, Oxfeld said the Levittown case provided the necessary push to get one going. "We need to build on this," he said. "The core of racial segregation in our communities is housing discrimination."

In fact, New Jersey people and places had always figured prominently in the history of the national ACLU. The organization was founded in 1920 in New York by Roger Baldwin, a liberal social reformer committed to free speech. During the early days of the ACLU Baldwin, a New Yorker with a farm in Sussex County, spent much of his time aiding labor unions in their struggle against government repression. Many of their battles to organize or strike were waged in the old factory towns of northern New Jersey.

In 1921 the ACLU published a pamphlet announcing its "free speech victory" in Passaic. In 1920, police had been harassing the Amalgamated Textile Workers by denying them permits for meetings. One night Passaic police barged into an "unauthorized" meeting of textile workers and turned off the lights. Union and ACLU officials calmly lit candles and took turns reading the state Constitution in protest.

Baldwin's actions on behalf of striking silk workers in Paterson led to his arrest in 1924. When he heard police were preventing the striking workers from meeting, he crossed the Hudson River and led a peaceful protest at City Hall. The protesters were listening to a recitation of the Bill of Rights when police grabbed an American flag belonging to two of them and ordered the crowd to disperse. Police arrested Baldwin and nine other men for "riotous" behavior. He was sentenced to a jail term of six months, although the state's highest court later threw out the conviction. Baldwin was also involved in a long and bitter strike in 1926 in Passaic.

Free-speech fights on behalf of organized labor continued to engage the ACLU well into the 1930s. "The issues of civil liberty in New Jersey, particularly in the industrial towns near New York, are many and constant," the ACLU's 1935 annual report stated. "Practically every strike involves attacks by police or courts upon picketing." The report also described emerging civil liberties problems among northern New Jersey's large population of Germans. Nazi-friendly groups were under attack and having trouble finding places to meet. The ACLU preached tolerance for the Friends of New Germany and its successor, the German American Bund, saying civil rights were guaranteed to all. The report said that German-Americans' right to meet and hold parades in the New Jersey towns lining the Hudson River had been "attacked" by police and injunctions.

Pro- and anti-Nazi groups actually came to blows in a Jersey City courtroom in 1934, when Union City officials sought an injunction against the Friends. The pro-Nazi club reportedly sang an anti-Semitic song to open meetings, beginning "Our greatest joy will come when Jewish blood flows through the streets," and boycotted local Jewish merchants. ACLU counsel Arthur Garfield Hays, himself a Jew, came to their defense despite their hateful ways, saying members had the right to express their prejudice. "It is better to have them express this animosity openly than have it suppressed and (go) underground," he told The New York Times.

The ACLU also lobbied the New Jersey Legislature against a bill making it a crime to spread propaganda inciting religious or racial hatred. The measure, commonly known as the Anti-Nazi Act, was adopted. When a test case involving 10 convicted Bund leaders came before the New Jersey Supreme Court, the justices declared the law unconstitutional, citing an ACLU amicus brief.

In those days Newark had its own committee of staunch civil libertarians, loosely allied with groups like the Committee of

As mayor of Jersey City, Frank "I am the Law" Hague banned leafleting, manhandled pickets and denied union organizers permits for meetings, claiming they were troublemaking Communists.
(Newark Public Library)

Industrial Organizations. Members lobbied legislators, monitored the Newark Police Department's anti-Communist "Red Squad," and defended the rights of pro-Nazi groups. The committee was directed by Nancy Cox, whose father was friendly with Roger Baldwin. Cox, 23, a Maplewood resident, was a former NYU student. Earlier she'd taught in a Pennsylvania steel town and been jailed there for distributing pro-labor leaflets without police permission. The Newark News, surprised to learn that her ancestors arrived before the American Revolution, wrote this headline for a feature story on her: "Busy for Civil Liberties Union, She Forgets Mayflower Ancestry."

Out of this era came one of the ACLU's biggest wins, *Hague v. Committee for Industrial Organization.* It started as a dispute between Frank "I am the Law" Hague, the dictatorial mayor of Jersey City, and organized labor. Hague, mayor from 1917 to 1937 and the Democratic boss of Hudson County, had begun his political career as a friend of the working man, but turned against labor after fights between union and non-union workers disrupted construction of the Pulaski Skyway. The conflict deepened when Hague embarked on a savage campaign against unions, especially the CIO, a militant association of unskilled workers.

The Wagner Act of 1935 restrained employers from interfering with union activity, but Hague used his executive power to drum activists out of town. He banned leafleting, manhandled pickets and denied union organizers permits for meetings on grounds they were troublemaking "Communists." One of the biggest fights between the mayor and the CIO occurred in 1937, when police arrested organizers and hauled them to the city line. In a radio address that December, ACLU director Roger Baldwin let Hague know he had gone too far. "Before we get through with Mayor Hague we will teach him a lesson in Americanism that he will never forget — that the defense of civil rights is not communism; (and) that loyalty to American institutions demands freedom of speech, press and assembly for all," Baldwin said.

The fight continued through 1938, when Hague threw perennial Socialist Party presidential candidate Norman Thomas out of town. Thomas was to address a crowd at Journal Square, but police hustled him into a car and drove him to the New York ferry. That was the last straw for the ACLU, which sought an injunction restraining Hague and other officials. After a colorful trial in Newark, District Court Judge William Clark — who compared Jersey City police to Adolf Hitler — permanently enjoined Hague and his men from interfering with peaceful public meetings, conducting illegal searches and "deporting" speakers. Attorneys Spaulding Frazer of Newark and Morris L. Ernst of New York were the victorious co-counsel for the ACLU and the C.I.O. Moments after the high court invalidated the ordinance restricting free speech, Arthur G. Hays, counsel for the ACLU, sent a telegraph to Jersey City police officials. It advised them that Norman Thomas and ACLU founder Roger Baldwin, previously personae non gratae, would be speaking at an open-air meeting in Jersey City the following Friday. Hague appealed, but in vain. On June 5, 1939, the U.S. Supreme Court ruled that he and Jersey City police had clearly violated the First Amendment.

The U.S. entered World War II on Dec. 8, 1941. Just as it had during World War I, the federal government gave itself broad authority to prosecute war critics and restrict civil liberties. The most glaring example was the roundup and internment of Japanese Americans living on the West Coast and in Hawaii. After the war, the FBI grew in size and power and expanded its surveillance on Communists and other left-wing groups and political parties. In New Jersey, as elsewhere in the country, left-leaning groups complained about government repression. In Newark, police made it hard for certain groups to hold meetings.

Things came to a head in 1947, when Emil Oxfeld learned Newark police were pressuring public hall owners not to rent space to "subversives." An acquaintance showed Oxfeld a notice he'd received from a hall owner, along with his cancelled contract. "I have been advised by the Newark Police that it is your intention to use the hall for Un-American activities," the letter read. Oxfeld was outraged. He organized a "free speech protest" on Nov. 20, 1947, at Newark's Mosque Theater, and took out newspaper ads inviting the public. Admission was 60 cents. Speakers included Roger Baldwin and other figures from the ACLU, local liberals and left-wingers and the chairmen of the New Jersey and New York Communist parties.

Attorney Emil Oxfeld, one of the founders of the ACLU-NJ, with biology teacher Estelle Laba, who was accused by the government of being a Communist. (Newark Public Library)

Emil Oxfeld

In 1960, Emil Oxfeld became the first president of the newly formed ACLU-NJ, a position he would hold for 25 years.

Oxfeld was a natural choice for the post, since he had been the ACLU presence on the ground in New Jersey since 1944, long before the affiliate formed. The need to have a state affiliate was great. Oxfeld had already defended teachers who lost their jobs for refusing to recite McCarthyist loyalty oaths and students who were banned from publishing articles criticizing the Hiroshima bombing in the school newspaper.

Throughout its first 25 years, the ACLU-NJ formed projects to defend the rights of specific groups: inner-city communities, women, farm workers, and prisoners. In 1970 Oxfeld established the ACLU-NJ's annual practice of honoring civil liberties leaders with awards, presenting the inaugural Roger N. Baldwin Civil Liberties Award to civil rights activist and New Jersey native son Paul Robeson. From 1960 to 1985, the number of ACLU members in New Jersey soared from 1,000 to 6,000.

In 1985, during the 25th anniversary of the ACLU-NJ, Oxfeld penned a concise yet inclusive overview of the organization's history.

"One of the interesting aspects of civil liberties work is that the present menace always looms larger than the ones that have been overcome," Oxfeld wrote. "I guess maybe that's the stimulation we need to try to stay forever young. I wonder how it will look after the next 25 years; I suspect not much different."

More than a thousand people showed up, according to news accounts. Oxfeld appealed to Gov. Alfred E. Driscoll and Newark Mayor Vincent Murphy to enforce the right of assembly for all groups — whether on the left or the right — no matter how unpopular their point of view. Driscoll responded by appointing a citizens Committee on Civil Rights.

Civil libertarians in New Jersey marked advances and setbacks alike in 1947. Voters approved a new state Constitution that greatly expanded civil rights. But the U.S. Supreme Court handed down a controversial ruling on church-state relations in a New Jersey case, *Everson v. Board of Education*. Arch R. Everson, a taxpayer in Ewing Township, sued his local school board over a law providing public funding for busing children to parochial schools. Everson prevailed in the lower court but was reversed on appeal, and the case went to the U.S. Supreme Court with the ACLU as a sponsor. The high court ruled that the "wall of separation" between church and state must be kept "high and impregnable," yet held that providing transportation to parochial schools was no different from providing police or fire protection. The muddled decision galvanized opinion on both sides of the issue.

Anti-Communist paranoia defined much of the following decade. The early 1950s came to be known as the McCarthy era, named after Joseph McCarthy, a Republican U.S. Senator from Wisconsin who led a virulent campaign against alleged Communists and spies. As chairman of the Senate Permanent Subcommittee on Investigations, McCarthy accused many kinds of people of treason or anti-government activity without conclusive evidence, creating a national atmosphere of fear and suspicion. McCarthy found support among conservative politicians and organizations, and even some newspapers. But he was not a one-man band. All levels of government, and some private employers, began demanding loyalty oaths from workers. The House Committee on Un-American Activities, which blacklisted Hollywood actors and producers in 1947, traveled around the country and subpoenaed suspected Communists to appear at hearings.

New Jersey saw its share of McCarthyism. The New Jersey Supreme Court, for example, upheld a decision by the Newark College of Engineering to fire a mechanical engineering teacher who refused to sign a loyalty oath. The Englewood Board of Education issued regulations censoring teaching materials it considered unpatriotic. Rutgers University announced automatic dismissal for any faculty member belonging to the Communist Party. The Newark Housing Authority tried to evict two tenants who declined to swear they did not belong to any of 200 organizations the U.S. Attorney General termed subversive.

In one of his more outrageous investigations, McCarthy went after a U.S. Army installation in Eatontown, where scientists and engineers developed radar and missile-guidance systems. The attack on the Army's Signal Center at Fort Monmouth began in October 1953. McCarthy said he'd found a trail of "extremely dangerous espionage" leading to Fort Monmouth that could destroy the country's "entire defense of atomic attack." His committee held secret hearings in New York and in Washington, D.C., grilling civilian employees for hours. It was true that convicted spy Julius Rosenberg — executed in June 1953 for passing secrets to the Soviet Union — had worked at the Eatontown facility during World War II. It was also possible that some of the scientists there in 1953 may have flirted with radical politics during their youth. But not a single spy was found. Nonetheless, 42 employees — 39 of them Jewish — were suspended from their jobs as security risks. Some were eventually reinstated, but others left, having lost their security clearances or their desire to remain in the Army, or both. Eight of them later filed civil actions seeking back pay and a court order clearing their reputation.

During the investigation, the maligned scientists and engineers had difficulty finding lawyers to defend them. One attorney who did represent some of them, Ira J. Katchen of Long Branch, told The New York Times in 1983 that national Jewish organizations kept their distance out of fear of "becoming involved" in the controversy. In a book about the ACLU, historian Samuel Walker writes that the organization had a fiercely anti-Communist faction between 1947 and 1954. As a result, he says, the ACLU "at times appeared hesitant" to act against civil liberties violations during the McCarthy period.

The other egregious example of McCarthyism in New Jersey took place in 1955, when the House Committee on Un-American Activities arrived in Newark to hunt down suspected Communists for four days of hearings. According to the committee, an unnamed FBI operative had revealed that 75 area professionals belonged to secret Communist clubs. Three Newark teachers subpoenaed to appear took the Fifth Amendment when asked if they had ever belonged to the Communist party, and were dismissed by the city Board of Education. Acting as a private attorney, Emil Oxfeld represented one of the three, biology teacher Estelle Laba. Five years later, the ACLU came to the aid of the other two, Robert Lowenstein and Perry Zimmerman. They were still fighting to get their jobs back.

On March 28, 1960, the ACLU in New York approved a constitution and by-laws for the new affiliate. The ACLU-NJ's goals were to advance civil liberties by defending freedom of speech, association and religion; due process, and equal treatment under the law. The first meeting, to which the public was invited, was June 16, 1960.

The ACLU already had 1,500 members in New Jersey, but Oxfeld wanted a stronger organization on the ground. He mined his personal and professional networks for people willing to serve on a board of trustees, and came up with 14. They included business people, attorneys, an Episcopalian clergyman, representatives of organized labor, two professors from Rutgers School of Law, a pediatrician, and a teacher, the lone woman.

"Emil and I were pretty good friends, and I knew many of the others personally. I knew their allegiances and their politics, if you will, and it was certainly the right group," Howard Levine, one of the original board members, recalled in 2011. "All of us came from basically liberal-thinking families, and we all had a sense of social responsibility. Emil was very dedicated to civil liberties and resented any encroachment. When he saw wrong, he was pre- pared to fight."

Board members were encouraged to raise the group's pro- file by giving talks to civic groups. Levine, a dress manufacturer, remembered chairing a debate on whether Communists ought to be allowed to teach. On another occasion, he delivered a lecture about the First Amendment at a meeting of a local Rotary Club. Levine didn't mind the exposure at all. He was used to public speaking, believed in the group's mission, and had lived through the McCarthy era. In the late 1940s, while teaching sociology at Brooklyn College, he had been asked to sign a loyalty oath. Offended, he declined to do so, and left. "When I was inducted into the Army, I swore I would be loyal to the United States. I thought that was enough."

Oxfeld had grown up in a working-class family in Newark, and gone to New York University and Harvard Law on scholarships. He was a gifted writer and speaker — he'd majored in English at college — and an aggressive lawyer. He was also a born promoter. Soon after the New Jersey affiliate was formed, Oxfeld invited two U.S. Supreme Court justices and the U.S. Attorney General to come to Newark and speak at an ACLU-NJ meeting. (They politely declined.)

At the time the affiliate was created, a handful of New Jersey cases were already on the national legal docket. One accused court-appointed counsel in three capital cases of inadequate representation of defendants. Another challenged the Freehold

Board of Education's policy of singing hymns in school. In the third case, the ACLU defended a Middlesex County man accused of running a pornographic film exchange.

Oxfeld made fighting censorship a top priority. A 1957 U.S. Supreme Court holding that obscene material was not protected under the First Amendment had fueled anti-obscenity campaigns in a number of New Jersey counties. In Paterson, the county prosecutor even deployed a group of high school students as junior investigators, sending them to scout for pornography at newsstands. Church-state relations were also high on Oxfeld's list. In 1962, following a U.S. Supreme Court ruling declaring school prayer unconstitutional, he embarked on a campaign to persuade Gov. Richard J. Hughes to end Bible reading and prayer in New Jersey schools.

For the first few years the New Jersey affiliate met in restaurants and trustees' living rooms. But in 1964 it was feeling flush enough to hire an executive director, Fred Barbaro, a social worker, and open an office at 31 Central Ave. in Newark. A push for county chapters came next. Chapters were formed in Bergen-Passaic, Monmouth, Morris and South Jersey in 1966. By the end of 1971, there were seven more. They became important building blocks for the fledging organization. Some functioned as full-fledged branches, raising funds, doing intake, and arranging representation for clients.

Former Princeton resident Estelle Kuhn, for example, ran the Mercer-Hunterdon chapter from 1973 until 1991 from a series of four offices, as a volunteer and later as a paid part-time manager. Kuhn jumped into the job as a full-time homemaker with a keen interest in social causes, when her youngest child was 13. Before long her office brought a civil action against the Trenton Board of Education for slashing the number of polling districts in a school board election. The lawsuit, which was successful, contended the new districts discriminated against blacks and Puerto Ricans by requiring them to travel long distances to cast their ballots.

From 1965 on, civil rights dominated the ACLU-NJ agenda. When Newark police shot and killed three residents under questionable circumstances, the ACLU-NJ began lobbying the city for a civilian police board. After members of the Students for a Democratic Society were arrested during a peaceful sit-in protesting slum housing, the ACLU-NJ dispatched a volunteer lawyer to appeal their conviction.

By 1966, Oxfeld considered the struggle for racial equality the affiliate's most important cause. One day that March, Oxfeld drove to the First Unitarian Church in Lincroft, in Monmouth County, to give a speech and drum up interest in a local chapter.

He wanted to talk about the civil rights issues confronting the state. Oxfeld announced that he planned to take legal action against a Monmouth County bus line that had refused to take anti-war protesters to a peace march in Washington five months earlier.

But some of those present were more interested in discussing pornography and censorship. State Sen. Mildred Barry Hughes and a local minister in the audience argued that obscenity was a threat to American morals. Hughes had been the principal sponsor of a bill banning the sale of "obscene literature" to anyone under 18.

Oxfeld bristled. Forget about trying to change morals, he told them. Much more important work lay ahead.

"Those who are professionally concerned with obscenity are making little or no contribution to the struggle for civil rights," Oxfeld said.

He was impatient with those who did not agree that the real threat to democracy was racial inequality — and he was right. The next year, a racial incident in Newark, the state's largest city, sparked six days of civil disturbances, resulting in the loss of 26 lives.

CHAPTER TWO

Social Upheaval

A Brawl Divides an Emotionally Raw City

Former ACLU-NJ Executive Director Henry di Suvero and then-wife Ramona Ripston allowed reporters to camp out at the ACLU's offices in Newark during the 1967 rebellion. (Newark Public Library)

The annual meeting of the American Civil Liberties Union of New Jersey in 1968 was expected to be an orderly affair, with the usual committee reports, old and new business, dinner, and speeches. But it was anything but peaceful. Members arriving at the Military Park Hotel in Newark encountered a group of rowdy pickets holding signs that read "ACLU Is Against Law and Order," "Untie Policemen's Hands" and "ACLU Are Pinks." The male pickets, in military fatigues and helmets, were members of the North Ward Citizens Committee, a vigilante group. The female pickets belonged to its female auxiliary, the Women's Organization for the Return of Law and Decency. As ACLU education director Rita D'Joseph passed by on her way into the hotel, she heard shouts of "Commie bastard!" and "Go get her!" and was shoved from behind. When she got inside she telephoned ACLU-NJ executive director Henry di Suvero, who rushed over. Then things turned violent.

Di Suvero asked a uniformed police officer to arrest the picket who had pushed D'Joseph, but the officer refused. Yet when a female picket accused di Suvero of assaulting her, an off-duty Newark cop stepped out from the picket line and arrested di Suvero. Vigilante leader Anthony Imperiale, a beefy former Marine and judo instructor, aimed a kick below his belt. Di Suvero, a lanky 32-year-old attorney who had never been arrested, was hauled off to jail.

The events of that day — April 20, 1968 — occurred nine months after the devastating Newark rebellion, but the wounds were still raw and the city racially polarized. Twenty-six people had died in the shootings — yet no one had been indicted or prosecuted in their deaths. People were fleeing to the suburbs. Ethnic whites like Imperiale feared they were losing their foothold in the city, and resented the ACLU-NJ for challenging the old order. As Newark burned, the ACLU-NJ office served as a headquarters for the media who came to Newark to cover the uprising.

The National Guard was called into Newark during the 1967 rebellion and was accused by the ACLU-NJ of shooting to kill. (From the Collections of the New Jersey Historical Society)

Anthony Imperiale, left, former Newark City Council member, shakes hands with former Mayor Kenneth Gibson. (Newark Public Library)

Di Suvero questioned the city's response to the crisis. When it was over, he sued the mayor and police chief.

During the rebellion the authorities and the press blamed anonymous "snipers" for the loss of life. Early on Gov. Richard Hughes spoke of a "criminal insurrection" and ordered in the New Jersey State Police and the National Guard. Di Suvero, listening to both sides, had taken a different tack. In a story published in The Newark News on July 15, 1967, after three days of rioting, di Suvero had blamed "police lawlessness" for contributing to the violence. He had expressed concern for the people of Newark — 18 were already dead, with another 850 injured — and criticized the way officials were handling arrests. Later, others came to his view, suggesting trigger-happy police and guardsmen may have inadvertently caused some of the deaths.

The ACLU-NJ remained in the public eye until the rioting ended. Together with Newark Legal Services it printed up thousands of flyers asking Newark residents to bring in physical evidence of police brutality, such as spent shells. Di Suvero offered his office to black leaders, and helped them put out a press release airing their grievances. He urged business leaders to issue a forceful statement calling for troops to be withdrawn. He got on the phone to the governor's legal staff and requested Hughes meet with black leaders. Di Suvero also shared eyewitness accounts of police brutality with political activist Tom Hayden, who published some of the accounts — without revealing names — in his 1967 book, "Rebellion in Newark." But that was not all. The ACLU-NJ also brought a stunning class-action lawsuit against the Newark Police Department, one of three rebellion-related civil actions filed against public officials that summer. The plaintiffs were 17 black Newark residents, starting with Marian Kidd, a welfare mother who lived in the heart of the riot area; the defendants were Hugh J. Addonizio, mayor of Newark; Dominick Spina, director of law and public safety; and Oliver Kelly, chief of police. *Kidd v. Addonizio* charged Newark police with depriving black residents of their constitutional rights by subjecting them to constant "violence, intimidation, and humiliation." It accused the police of beating blacks for no reason, habitually referring to them with "obscene racial epithets" and spying on those who attempted to exercise their civil rights. And it alleged that police — and "some state troopers and national guardsmen" — intensified this behavior during the rebellion, deliberately destroying black-owned property and shooting to kill. Twenty-four of the 26 who died during the rebellion were African-American.

"Plaintiffs and the members of their class have for many years not enjoyed full and equal participation in the political, economic and social affairs of the City of Newark," the complaint stated. "The agents and employees of defendants . . . have attempted to teach plaintiffs and members of their class that (they) are beings of an inferior order."

Newark officials greeted the accusations with derision. So did Anthony Imperiale, the leader of the North Ward Citizens Committee. Imperiale formed the controversial vigilante group after the riots, saying it was needed to keep invaders out of the largely Italian-American North Ward. His militancy turned him into a minor celebrity overnight. Imperiale was a deliberate race baiter who blamed "Communist" conspirators and radicals for turning blacks against whites. In 1968, he was elected to the Newark City Council as a symbol of white backlash. In 1969, he toned down the rhetoric and successfully ran for the New Jersey General Assembly.

It's hard to imagine anyone less like Imperiale than the executive director of the ACLU-NJ. Di Suvero had come to Newark after working for the ACLU in New York. He had never before set foot in New Jersey. He was born in China, the son of a Catholic mother and a Jewish father who worked for the Italian diplomatic corps. When World War II broke out, his father was ordered to return to Italy, but chose instead to emigrate to California and become an American citizen. Di Suvero was educated in California and had planned to return there, but extended his stay in New York when his brother, Mark — later a famous sculptor — was injured in a construction accident. Once he decided to take the position in Newark, he moved to Weehawken with his wife, Ramona Ripston, and three children.

The fracas at the Military Park Hotel, where he was arrested, occurred a year later, in 1968. Di Suvero ended up in jail, facing a slew of serious charges. His lawyer was Leonard Weinglass, a young Newark attorney loosely connected to Rutgers School of Law. (Later in his career Weinglass defended a number of controversial figures, including Daniel Ellsberg, and Kathy Boudin, a member of the radical Weather Underground.) After his release from jail di Suvero filed a countersuit charging police with failure to protect him and Rita D'Joseph. He also alleged Newark police were in cahoots with the picketing vigilantes.

Di Suvero was eventually exonerated. A grand jury found no cause for indictment, and a municipal court judge cleared him of the lesser charges he faced. Di Suvero credited the testimony of a businessman for his good fortune. The man had been on his way to a meeting at the Military Park Hotel when, by chance, he witnessed the scuffle. After reading a one-sided newspaper account of the tussle, he contacted the ACLU-NJ and volunteered to be a witness. And he testified it was di Suvero who had been assaulted.

"It was a beautiful thing. Otherwise, it would have been my word against that of two or three cops," di Suvero said in a 2011 interview.

"He was totally independent, with no connection to the ACLU, just terribly offended by what he saw, namely someone walking peacefully through and being jumped on." (In an unexpected post-script to the story, the officer who arrested di Suvero later asked the ACLU-NJ to represent him in an unrelated dismissal complaint. "We were very receptive to his discharge complaint," said Stephen Nagler, who succeeded di Suvero as director.)

Di Suvero left the ACLU-NJ in 1968 to work for the National Emergency Civil Liberties Committee in New York, a group formed during the McCarthy era. He eventually left the U.S. and settled in Australia, where he practiced law. After retiring from the law, he became a playwright. Many years later, and miles away, di Suvero is still rewarded by his time in Newark; he proudly dis-plays a plaque given to him 43 years earlier by the Newark chapter of the Congress of Racial Equality. "Presented to Henry di Suvero, In Appreciation for Legal & Humanitarian Services Rendered To The Black Community," it reads.

Ripston eventually became executive director of the ACLU of Southern California, where she served 38 years. In an interview in 2010, she said her time in Newark heightened her awareness of police brutality in impoverished cities.

Newark's deadly rebellion was not unexpected. Civil rights activists had warned that violence was likely that summer, but city officials played down fears and said they could handle any prob-lems. "Newark had been tagged as a likely riot spot this summer, so the (New Jersey) ACLU together with the Newark Legal Services Project had, weeks before the riots, set up a team of lawyers to be called upon in just such an emergency," an ACLU staffer in New York wrote nine days after the riots.

The city exemplified every imaginable urban ill. Taxes were high, schools were decaying, and manufacturing jobs were desert-

Ramona Ripston

One day Ramona Ripston, a housewife and mother of three children, walked into the New York ACLU's office and signed up to volunteer. They liked her work so much that they offered her a paid position as a fundraiser and editor. But when she told her husband about the job offer, he demanded she turn it down and stay at home.

Ripston took the job and left the husband. It was the start of her storied career as one of the most outspoken and respected voices on civil rights issues in the nation.

In the 1960s, Ripston urged her new husband, activist and lawyer Henry di Suvero, to apply to become executive director of the ACLU-NJ. When di Suvero landed the job, Ripston worked alongside him, handling press inquiries and raising money for the affiliate.

On the morning of July 12, 1967, news broke of rioting and looting in the streets of Newark. Already on the road for a trip to the beach, they immediately turned the car around and headed to the ACLU's office on Academy Street, where they watched flames lick the city's streets.

"It really made a great impression on me," Ripston said. "There was so much poverty in Newark. The police were very antagonistic towards blacks. My experience in Newark helped me want to do something about police behavior and cities with mayors that didn't care about poor people."

In 1972, Ripston became executive director of the Southern California affiliate, becoming the first woman in the country to assume a leadership role in the ACLU.

ing the city. Most of its black citizens lived in the Central Ward, where absentee landlords let buildings crumble, white merchants charged outrageous prices, and Newark City Hospital provided notoriously poor care. By 1963, young civil rights activists had begun protesting conditions. At a meeting that year ACLU-NJ trustees took note of the rising number of civil rights violations, and voted 7-5 to join the Essex County Coordinating Committee, a coalition advocating for racial equality. The group included the NAACP, the Congress of Racial Equality and the Urban League. Relations between the black community and the Newark Police Department were poor. A string of suspicious police shootings led the ACLU-NJ to begin pressing for a civilian police review board. In the first of these cases, a suspect supposedly died after striking his head on a steel file cabinet; in the second, a fleeing suspect was killed when a "warning shot" ricocheted off a street light and hit him. But the most notorious suspicious death occurred on June 12, 1965, when 22-year-old Lester Long was shot and killed after being stopped for a traffic violation. The official explanation of his death made no sense. Fred Barbaro, then ACLU-NJ executive director, lobbied hard for a civilian police review board, but the city administration was adamantly opposed. Negotiations ended with Mayor Addonizio promising to refer future complaints of excessive force to the FBI. In the meantime, complaints about police brutality mounted. Many believe the police beating of a black cab driver, John Smith, touched off the riots.

In *Kidd v. Addonizio*, the first ACLU-NJ lawsuit filed after the riots, volunteer attorney Morton Stavis devised a novel legal strategy that merged civil rights law with a request for a receiver to run the Newark Police Department. Receiverships were typically used in commercial cases, not civil rights cases. The lawsuit was dismissed in 1972. By then Addonizio was in federal prison, having been convicted of extortion. But *Kidd v. Addonizio* had a potent and lasting effect, according to former ACLU-NJ board member Robert Curvin, one of the plaintiffs and chairman of the Newark chapter of CORE from 1962 to 1964. "It was really a pioneering effort," he said years later. "It represented the first serious effort to legally challenge the city's administration and operation of the Newark Police Department. And we had this incredible battery of lawyers who were all basically free. They were totally dedicated."

In a deposition filed in the case, Curvin provided detail about brutality during his CORE days. Although he had a good relationship with one police inspector, most officers treated him disrespectfully. At one demonstration, he objected when an officer rammed his nightstick into a protestor's ribs. According to Curvin's deposition, the cop replied, "You black son of a bitch, if I didn't have this badge on I would kick your ass." Another plaintiff in the case, the Rev. Dennis Westbrooks, said police grabbed him in a chokehold and threw him out of a hospital when he attempted to minister to people hurt during the riots. A third, Ozell Brown, whose wife was killed that week, said he overheard police say, "Let's kill all these black bastards before they kill us."

After *Kidd v. Addonizio* the ACLU-NJ filed two more lawsuits relating to police brutality. The first came on the heels of a civil disturbance in Plainfield, also in July 1967. On the third night of violence there, a patrolman named John Gleason critically wounded a looter. A street mob then pounced on Gleason, who was white, and killed him with his service revolver. That same night 46 semiautomatic weapons and ammunition were stolen from a gun factory nearby, and police worried the guns would make their way into the riot zone. Gov. Hughes, who had declared a state of emergency in Plainfield three days earlier, ordered armed troops to conduct a house-by-house search of the city's black neighborhoods. Occupants were told to get out of their homes by shouts from the street, and held at gunpoint while their homes were searched. If no one was home, police broke down the door. According to state officials, three rifles turned up in the search.

The ACLU-NJ sued Gov. Hughes, contending police should have obtained search warrants. The lawsuit, *Adams v. Hughes*, sought $1 million in damages. Adams was the name of one of the people whose homes were ransacked. Hughes justified the searches on the grounds that they occurred during a state of emergency, but settled out of court for $40,000 in damages, to be divided among the ACLU-NJ and individual plaintiffs. Each of the 63 plaintiffs received a minimum of $100, with the largest payment going to a woman nursing her baby when state troopers burst into her apartment.

In the third riot-related lawsuit, *Wynn v. Byrne*, the ACLU-NJ sought to restrain Essex County Prosecutor Brendan Byrne from proceeding with prosecutions. Wynn was the name of one of those arrested during the Newark riots. This lawsuit alleged the authorities rushed to prosecution, denying defendants due process and assembling mostly white grand juries. "At stake is not only confidence of the Negro community in the fair administration of justice, but the very fabric of justice itself," the complaint stated. The ACLU-NJ lost this one, but it was right to have questioned the justice system. In the end, no one was held accountable for the deaths of the 26 people who lost their lives in the riots.

The late 1960s were a time of social upheaval. Anti-war sentiment pervaded the country; a Gallup poll in August 1968 found 53 percent of those surveyed believed the Vietnam War was a tragic blunder. The assassinations of Martin Luther King Jr. and U.S. Sen. Robert F. Kennedy deepened fears about civil unrest and extremists. Confrontations between young people and police became commonplace. Young people who grew long hair, smoked marijuana, or embraced the so-called sexual revolution were viewed as threats to the social order. Government responded by clamping down on personal freedoms and initiating domestic surveillance of the sort usually reserved for intelligence agents of foreign countries.

The ACLU-NJ, hit with a barrage of complaints, moved from an emphasis on amicus briefs to direct representation of clients. In

High school student Micah Bertin,
left, and ACLU-NJ cooperating
attorney Jack Wysoker appear in
court to challenge a school district's
decision to ban Bertin from his
graduation because his sideburns
were considered excessively long.
Bertin appealed, prevailed and
delivered a valedictory address
about fighting for a principle.
(Newark Public Library)

1967 its team of volunteer attorneys handled 26 cases. By 1970, the number was up to 300. The mayor of Linden tried to block black students and their parents from staging a demonstration. Two Bergen County towns wanted to bar peace groups from marching in Memorial Day parades. The city of Elizabeth ordered anyone passing out leaflets to get a permit. The Edison Township Board of Education barred high school senior Micah Bertin — president of the graduating class, and a top-notch student — from graduation because his sideburns, ending at the midpoint of each earlobe, were "excessively long" and "disruptive." A municipal judge in Willingboro chastised a man for coming to court in a dashiki. For the ACLU-NJ, which intervened successfully in every one of these cases, it was a busy time.

Wherever one looked, there seemed to be clashes. Civil libertarians even argued among themselves. A serious rift developed between the ACLU and some of its state affiliates, including New Jersey, over the federal government's prosecution of Benjamin Spock, the pediatrician and bestselling author of "Baby and Child Care." Spock and four other well-known anti-war activists had been charged with conspiracy to aid draft resisters. Despite the free-speech issues involved, the national ACLU board voted against directly representing Spock, saying defense arguments were likely to challenge the legality of the war itself. ACLU-NJ

Rita & Bill Bender

In 1968, one year after the streets of Newark erupted in violence and police brutality, a new office called the Community Legal Action Workshop opened quietly along a tattered stretch of Springfield Avenue.

The ACLU-NJ's storefront office sent a message to residents in the neighborhood struck hardest by the rebellion : They had legal recourse for police brutality and misconduct. There was a tiny staff of two —Rita Bender, then a recent graduate of Rutgers School of Law-Newark, and a receptionist. Bender fielded inquiries from residents who wandered into the office. Some shared stories about police misconduct, while others simply wanted to talk about the goings-on in the neighborhood.

"We would get into discussions about what was happening to their kids in schools, or in the streets," she said. "The community was very, very emotionally raw."

Bender and her husband, Bill, got involved with the ACLU-NJ while they were law students together. In the immediate aftermath of the rebellion , the couple worked on a team of young attorneys alongside Frank Askin, Oliver Lofton and Annamay Sheppard, who volunteered to represent victims of indiscriminate police roundups, police abuse, or wrongful criminal charges.

"It was necessary and important," Bill Bender said of his time working with the ACLU. "You couldn't live in that community at that time and not get involved."

president Emil Oxfeld boldly attacked the national board's position in The New York Times, calling it "narrow-minded, backward-looking, and a repudiation of the origins of the ACLU." "We in New Jersey will continue to extend our resources to provide full protection in this time of war crisis to those who are advocates of draft resistance, or who are otherwise engaged in constitutionally protected activities," Oxfeld wrote in the ACLU-NJ newsletter, The Civil Liberties Reporter. "We will continue to adhere to the fundamental ACLU principle that the content of speech is irrelevant to our decision in the handling of a case. We are confident that this position will ultimately prevail, even at the national level."

Oxfeld was right. The national board did change its mind, although Spock and his co-defendants secured other counsel. The famous pediatrician was convicted, but his conviction was later set aside.

By 1968, opposition to the war threatened the Selective Service system. Draft resisters filed for conscientious-objector status, didn't report for induction, or tried to claim disability. Soldiers went AWOL, or fled to Canada, and college students demonstrated against military recruiters. Gen. Lewis B. Hershey, director of the National Selective Service, issued a directive threatening anti-war protesters with the loss of their draft deferments or immediate induction. His actions triggered lawsuits all over the country, including New Jersey.

In January 1968, the ACLU-NJ filed a federal lawsuit on behalf of 12 New Jersey residents who had turned in their draft cards in symbolic protest against the war and whose draft classifications consequently were changed. The plaintiffs, three of whom had ministerial exemptions, ranged in age from 20 to 31. After turning in their cards — Selective Service regulations required men to keep them on their persons at all times — their draft status was changed to 1-A, making them available for immediate military service. Their suit attacked the Hershey directive as a violation of free speech, and asked the court to enjoin their induction into the armed forces. The judge in the case agreed

First Amendment issues were involved, but declined to review the reclassifications.

In a parallel case, a federal appeals court ruled the Hershey letter could indeed have a chilling effect on free speech. The U.S. Supreme Court also ruled — in a case involving a young man denied conscientious-objector status who threw his draft card at a federal marshal — that Selective Service lacked the legal authority to speed up the induction of war protesters.

Given the extent of anti-war feeling, the ACLU-NJ established a Selective Service Project under the direction of Rutgers Law student Jeffrey Fogel. He organized a series of seminars for ACLU-NJ volunteer attorneys on Selective Service law and helped set up draft-information centers to counsel draft-eligible men.

Herbert Waldman, another Rutgers Law student involved in the project, said clients were one of two types. "There were a lot of young men who, for one reason or another — usually their position on the war — didn't want to go in. There were also men in who wanted to get out," he said. Waldman knew draft law from having worked for a Quaker group in Philadelphia. His toughest cases involved soldiers denied conscientious-objector status. Many were already in infantry training by the time they realized they couldn't kill. "I remember several cases where young men in that situation had orders to ship out. A lot of time we'd have to go into federal court and try to block their orders," Waldman recalled. "These cases got very tricky. The issue would be, was it properly denied? Was the belief religious? Did the person really believe it? Is the conscientious objection to all war?"

Soon the ACLU-NJ had a reputation for assisting soldiers. In 1969, a G.I. in solitary confinement at Fort Dix for deserting smuggled out a letter alleging that guards beat up anti-war prisoners in the stockade. The ACLU-NJ publicized the letter and others like it, but did not succeed in getting Congress to investigate. It also sought to persuade an Army colonel at Fort Dix to allow an anti-war newspaper to circulate at the base.

Stephen Nagler, who took over as director in 1968, was a former Peace Corps teacher in Africa and a former assistant director of CORE's Scholarship, Education and Defense Fund for Racial Equality. He was determined that the ACLU-NJ take on every clear rights violation that came its way and vastly expanded the legal docket. Nagler was also a talented fundraiser and grant writer who took the organization in many new directions. It opened branches in Camden, Trenton, Atlantic City and New Brunswick, and launched a series of special projects.

The first such project, dubbed a "ghetto office," was actually set up under his predecessor. It was called CLAW, short for Community Legal Action Workshop. The idea came from the national ACLU, which had proposed opening inner-city storefronts in 1964. The Southern California ACLU was the first to do so, after the Watts riot in 1965.

New Jersey was next, in 1968.

"Our relations with the black community are as good as any white group's can be," the ACLU-NJ wrote in a funding proposal at the time. "We receive requests for assistance from civil rights leaders, ministers, social workers, and the only black officeholder in the city. . . . Newark is controlled by an old line machine, now in the hands of the dominant white group, the Italians. The power structure is not only unresponsive but inept. The Police Department reaction to the riots has been to take a 'hard line.'" The New Jersey affiliate said a ghetto office would allow it to deepen its reach beyond downtown.

CLAW began operations at 542 Springfield Ave., the heart of the riot area, under Rita Bender, a recent Rutgers Law graduate and former field worker in Mississippi for CORE. She was also the widow of Michael Schwerner, one of three young civil rights workers murdered near Philadelphia, Miss., in the summer of 1964. The office, a one-lawyer operation with a secretary, focused on civil liberties deprivations affecting the poor. "The program is not intended as a substitute for the Newark Legal Services program, but as a supplement," Bender said in an interview published in the September 1968 edition of the ACLU-NJ's Civil Liberties Reporter. "(It) will concentrate intensively on developing legal remedies to basic problems which plague the 'ghetto'. This city is in need of drastic measures if it is to be saved from official ruin."

CLAW participated in some large lawsuits. It sued on behalf of minorities seeking employment at two major, federally financed construction projects in Newark. It sued to enjoin state welfare aid cuts, and it sued to overturn the state's abortion law. While it looked for patterns and large classes of plaintiffs, it also represented individuals whose personal liberties had been violated. When a Newark couple complained that an undercover police narcotic squad had stormed their apartment by mistake — holding them and their children at gunpoint, while going through their possessions — CLAW sued in federal court, seeking a broad injunction against the practice, as well as damages for the individual plaintiffs.

CLAW remained open for business for eight years, longer than any other ACLU storefront law office. Its last director was Bernard Freamon, who took over after graduating from Rutgers Law in 1972. "It was a real bona fide storefront law office, and I was very proud to be there," said Freamon, a professor at the Seton Hall University School of Law since 1979. He represented prisoners, mental patients who had been institutionalized and then forgotten, people hurt during a 1974 riot by Puerto Ricans, and residents protesting poor government services. One case he remembered very clearly involved an initiative by police to fingerprint every eighth-grader at a local school. "They had a fingerprint that an expert said was from a juvenile, so they wanted to fingerprint all the children. That's known as a writ of assistance. Another word is dragnet," Freamon said. "It's banned in the Constitution — the Fourth Amendment doesn't allow it. That's one of the things the people fought the American Revolution for." Without going to court, he persuaded the police department to back down.

The 1960s ended on a high note for the ACLU-NJ, with a victory in the country's first police surveillance lawsuit in New Jersey Superior Court. Or so it seemed.

In April 1968, with memories of the Newark and Plainfield riots still fresh, New Jersey Attorney General Arthur Sills issued a memorandum entitled "Civil Disorders — The Role of Local, County and State Government." Sills' memo advised local police to develop secret files on activists attending any "civil disturbance, riot, rally, protest, demonstration, etc.," and collect information about the group involved (such as "left wing, right wing, civil rights, militant, nationalistic, pacifist, religious, black power, Ku Klux Klan, extremist, etc."). Files on individuals were to include information on personal relationships and finances — it did not matter if there was no reason to suspect them of violating a law.

The directive was promptly challenged by the ACLU-NJ, which asked the court to halt the investigations and order existing dossiers destroyed. Volunteer attorney Frank Askin brought the action against Hudson County and the Jersey City Police Department, with Sills as co-defendant. He argued that secret files violated constitutional guarantees of free speech and assembly, and Judge Robert A Matthews agreed. The judge called Sills' directive "inherently dangerous" and said it would tend to inhibit advocates for social and political change.

But the victory was short-lived. On appeal the New Jersey Supreme Court ruled that state and local law enforcement agencies had every right to keep files on demonstrators, whether peaceful or violent. "Lawlessness has a tyranny of its own," the court said in a unanimous decision, "and it would be folly to deprive the government of its power to deal with that tyranny because of a figment of a fear that government itself may run amok."

Askin, who had thought he had a solid case, was surprised. He was also disappointed. The case had a particular resonance for him. At the age of 17 he joined the Communist Party in his home, Baltimore, and became a party organizer one year later. The Communists he knew back then were not violent people, but it was 1950, the height of anti-Communist paranoia. The FBI opened a file on him, followed him around and, on occasion, accosted him. Years later, when studying the First Amendment in law school, he became incensed. "I thought, 'Where did the FBI get the right to start a file on me? I was never accused of a crime. I was just exercising my right of speech and free association,' " he said.

He got another run at the issue when the national ACLU asked him to challenge a U.S. Army surveillance program of anti-war and civil rights activists. That case, filed in Washington, D.C., went before the U.S. Supreme Court. Askin lost again. The justices upheld the constitutionality of military surveillance of civilians in a 5-4 decision, with Associate Justice William Rehnquist, a former member of President Richard Nixon's Justice Department, casting the deciding vote. The majority also pointed out that the plaintiffs had failed to establish that they suffered any particular harm.

"When I filed these cases initially I thought the Warren Court decisions were on my side. The 'chilling effect' was significant. But the handwriting was on the wall. A different dynamic was going on," Askin recalled many years later. "The courts were getting more conservative."

CHAPTER THREE

Knocking Down Barriers

A Widower Takes on the Social Security Administration

Stephen Wiesenfeld sued the federal government for denying him Social Security survivor's benefits after his wife died. The U.S. Supreme Court ruled in his favor in 1975. (The Associated Press)

Stephen Wiesenfeld wasn't angry when he wrote to his local newspaper. He was sad and offended by the unfairness of the situation, but he had not been terribly surprised. When his wife died giving birth to their first child, the Social Security Administration denied him a benefit it routinely paid widowed mothers. Their baby, Jason, was now six months old. When the paper ran a story about widowers raising children, Stephen saw an opening to tell the world about the injustice. He knew there had to be others like him.

If you had told Wiesenfeld then that his letter would prompt one of the biggest gender discrimination cases of the 1970s, that the nation's highest court would rule in his favor, or that his lawyer — Ruth Bader Ginsburg — would officiate one day at Jason's wedding as an associate justice of the U.S. Supreme Court herself, he might have laughed. He was idealistic, but a realist, too.

"Your article about widowed men last week prompts me to point out a serious inequality in the Social Security law. It has been my misfortune to discover that a man cannot collect Social Security benefits as a woman can," he wrote to The Home News of New Brunswick in November 1972. Wiesenfeld, a 29-year-old computer consultant with four degrees, went on to explain that he and Paula, a teacher, had reversed traditional spousal roles, and that he did most of the homemaking. Yet Social Security had denied him "mother's insurance" benefits. "My son can collect benefits but I, because I am not a woman homemaker, cannot. I wonder if Gloria Steinem knows about this?"

Wiesenfeld mentioned Steinem, a leading feminist voice of the era, because he believed federal policy repudiated the value of Paula's life and work. The monthly benefit was only about $200, but it would have helped him work limited hours while caring for Jason. "It was the principle that irked me. It had nothing to do with money for me," he said years later. "What was important to

Ruth Bader Ginsburg, later a U.S. Supreme Court justice, handled several sex discrimination cases for the ACLU-NJ and represented Stephen Wiesenfeld's successful bid for Social Security survivor's benefits after his wife died. (Rutgers School of Law)

me was what happened to the money Paula paid into the system. She had been paying the maximum for seven years. All of a sudden, the money was lost. What was the purpose of paying in?"

Wiesenfeld's letter to the editor grabbed the attention of Phyllis Zatlin Boring, a Spanish professor at Rutgers University in New Brunswick. She brought it up with Ruth Bader Ginsburg, a professor at Rutgers School of Law in Newark from 1963 to 1972. Boring knew Ginsburg from a class-action lawsuit Ginsburg had joined, alleging Rutgers paid female faculty less than their male colleagues.

"Phyllis called me and said, 'That's not right, is it? Isn't there something in the Constitution about that?'" Ginsburg told an interviewer in 2007. She told Boring to get in touch with Wiesenfeld and have him contact the American Civil Liberties Union of New Jersey. Ginsburg had handled a number of sex discrimination cases for the New Jersey affiliate during the late 1960s. Although she began her career at Rutgers as an expert in Swedish civil law, she ended up specializing in gender discrimination in the U.S.

A month or two later, Ginsburg telephoned Wiesenfeld herself. From her perspective, his case represented a fantastic opportunity. The facts were not in dispute. The situation was very touching and very real. To top it off, the plaintiff was male. "We were trying to show that arbitrary differentials based on sex hurt everybody," Ginsburg said.

In March 1973, Ginsburg and the ACLU-NJ sued the government in federal District Court in Newark. Wiesenfeld's complaint alleged that the government's "mother's insurance benefit" denied him the due process and equal protection guaranteed by the Fifth Amendment to the Constitution. By then Ginsburg was at Columbia University Law School and director of the new Women's Rights Project of the ACLU. Jane Z. Lifset, a volunteer attorney for the ACLU-NJ and its liaison to the Women's Rights Project, became the attorney of record. She was thrilled to have a role in the case.

Bill Buckman

Bill Buckman was standing near an exit on the New Jersey Turnpike, thumb stretched midair, looking to hitch a ride from New York City to Cherry Hill. A State Police vehicle veered off the highway and pulled directly in front of Buckman.

The troopers smiled and laughed as they inched the car closer to the 16-year-old's knees, forcing him to walk backwards slowly.

The incident hardened Buckman's beliefs about government — that it could be arbitrary and abusive, especially if its power went unchecked. The Turnpike would also be the focal point for a case he argued that would be one of the most significant in the history of both the ACLU-NJ and New Jersey.

In 1970, Buckman opened an ACLU office in Atlantic City and became the youngest member on its board of trustees. In 1999, after fielding complaints from black motorists harassed on the state's roadways, Buckman would play a key role in pressuring New Jersey to admit the harassment was racially motivated. He and a team of other ACLU-NJ attorneys successfully won a settlement on behalf of 12 motorists who were stopped on the Turnpike because of their skin color.

"The racial profiling work is the most significant that I've done with the ACLU," Buckman said. "I felt that we were doing the right thing — that people of color had the right to travel the highways of New Jersey without being stopped, endangered, humiliated and harassed."

"There was just no doubt that the case would be extremely important, groundbreaking. It was a head-on rejection of women's work," said Lifset, who drafted Wiesenfeld's affidavits. "One of Ruth's strategies was to show men that discrimination hurt them as much as it hurt women, and this is exactly what this did. It was a man getting screwed. It was perfect."

The case was heard by a three-judge panel in Trenton. For technical reasons, no matter who won, an appeal would proceed directly to the U.S. Supreme Court. The panel ruled in Wiesenfeld's favor on Dec. 14, 1973. The first person notified, in those pre-Internet, pre-fax days, was Lifset, who found the decision stuffed in a thick letter-sized envelope in her mailbox. Wiesenfeld heard the news from a neighbor who'd been listening to the radio. By this time he had a bicycle store in Highland Park, where he could work while watching Jason, now 1½ years old. He had quit a higher-paying consulting job to qualify for the benefit, in case he prevailed. The government appealed.

Weinberger v. Wiesenfeld came before the U.S. Supreme Court in January 1975. Weinberger was Casper Weinberger, secretary of the U.S. Department of Health, Education and Welfare. Ginsburg insisted that Wiesenfeld, who traveled to Washington for the occasion, sit directly next to her during oral arguments. When they talked the night before, Ginsburg laid out her strategy. With only eight justices hearing the case, she was worried about a split decision. (Justice William O. Douglas was ill and did not take part). "She felt she'd be lucky if we won," he recalled. "She said she was going to present her argument in language that (Justice) Potter Stewart had written in other decisions, and she was going to look at him the entire time. She thought his vote would determine whether she could win or lose."

Ginsburg underestimated her powers of persuasion. The court ruled 8-to-0 that the Social Security provision denying Wiesenfeld benefits was unconstitutional. Congress intended "to provide children deprived of one parent with the opportunity for the personal attention of the other," irrespective of sex, the court said.

The monthly benefit was then $275. The court's ruling applied automatically to all widowers who qualified, of whom there were many. After the lower court victory, men like Wiesenfeld wrote to Lifset for advice on how to proceed with their own claims. "The additional income will mean a great deal to me," widower Elwood Freymire wrote from Pennsylvania. His wife Marilynn had died of a brain tumor eight years after they were married, leaving him the sole parent of a daughter, Kim.

With the case over, Wiesenfeld and his son moved to Florida, where his parents were living. "I wanted to adjust my lifestyle so I could afford to stay home with Jason on the money I had, plus the Social Security," he said. When Jason was nine, Wiesenfeld started a software design business outside the home. As the child grew older, he absorbed his family's story, piece by piece. He went to college and law school, married, and had three children of his own.

The Wiesenfeld case was a huge victory for the ACLU-NJ. It promoted gender equality and questioned the stereotypical view of marriage. But it also demonstrated the symbiotic relationship between the New Jersey affiliate and Rutgers School of Law in Newark. The ACLU-NJ identified and sponsored litigation; law school faculty and student volunteers added valuable expertise and human resources.

By the mid-1970s Rutgers law school had a fair number of students who viewed the law as more than a reliable means of earning money. There were also more women, minorities and older students than at most law schools. Professors like Ginsburg and Arthur Kinoy, long a force in the civil rights movement, were attracting the next generation of public-interest law students. The curriculum offered clinics that allowed students to address important societal needs while studying the law: the Urban Legal

Frank Askin founded the Constitutional Litigation Clinic, which ushered through a generation of public interest attorneys who worked closely with the ACLU-NJ in the 1970s. (Rutgers School of Law)

Clinic, created in response to the Newark riots by Professor Annamay Sheppard; the Constitutional Litigation Clinic, begun by Professor Frank Askin, and the Women's Rights Litigation Clinic, directed by Professor Nadine Taub. Rutgers even had a nickname, The People's Electric Law School, affectionately conferred by left-leaning students in reference to writer Tom Wolfe's "The Electric Kool-Aid Acid Test," a book about the 1960s counterculture.

Like others of this era, Jeffrey Fogel, who graduated from Rutgers in 1969, viewed the law as a tool for social change. He worked for the ACLU-NJ through most of law school. "I was thrilled to be part of it. I was somewhat radicalized at college, and went to law school with the notion of changing the world," he said. Fogel had a long run with the affiliate, starting as a volunteer the summer after his first year of law school. Soon he was working part-time on actual cases, drafting complaints and writing briefs. He even became a plaintiff after graduating, in a lawsuit accusing the New Jersey State Police of systematically stopping and searching long-haired men on the New Jersey Turnpike and other state highways. Hippies, in other words.

With his big beard and wild, frizzy hair, Fogel certainly looked the part. He worked at a law firm of radical young lawyers known as the Newark Law Commune. One weekend day, police stopped him and a law partner in their Volkswagen van for no apparent reason on the Garden State Parkway. They had driven to a VW dealer to buy some parts for the van, which they owned jointly, and were on their way back north. "When we got stopped, the trooper ordered my partner out of the car, then me," Fogel said. "Then he stepped in and started searching the shelf. I said, 'You can't do that.' He said, 'What are you, a wise guy?' I said, 'I may be, but I'm also a lawyer.' "

Harassment by police was part and parcel of the 1970s, but it wasn't just police who violated people's constitutional rights. Other institutions also restricted personal freedoms. School administrators censored student publications. Towns adopted curfews and "anti-loitering" ordinances. Many of the older generation seemed to be at war with people under 30, especially after the 1970 Kent State University shootings in which four students were killed when members of the Ohio National Guard fired shots into a crowd of student protesters who had ignored an order to disperse. Liberal Democrats started a movement to dump President Richard Nixon. All these conflicts contributed to a growth in ACLU membership, both nationally and in New Jersey. In 1972 the New Jersey affiliate

As an ACLU-NJ cooperating attorney Annamay Sheppard helped female athletes, including Abbe Seldin, win the right to play on all-boys teams in the 1970s. (Rutgers School of Law)

reported having the second largest legal docket of any ACLU unit in the country, with 343 cases on the docket.

The long-haired traveler case, filed in federal court by the ACLU-NJ and the Constitutional Litigation Clinic at Rutgers at the close of 1970, was the first lawsuit charging the state police with "profiling" drivers. Profiling is the practice of singling out members of specific groups — usually by appearance — and searching them for evidence of criminal activity. Profiling came to be associated with skin color, but in 1970 the claim was that state police targeted men with long hair. The 37 plaintiffs were college students, law students, lawyers and teachers who alleged troopers had violated their constitutional rights by stopping them and searching for marijuana or narcotics. The 37 stops had produced 10 arrests, half of which were for marijuana possession.

The long-haired travelers lost. Their lawsuit had such a long and complex history — two federal judges died while hearing the case — that it wasn't until 1976 that the U.S. Supreme Court determined the outcome in a ruling in another case. In that case, alleging harassment of blacks by Philadelphia police, the Supreme Court ruled federal courts had no power to oversee local police, even when accused of unconstitutional conduct. The appeals court weighing the case acknowledged that troopers showed "callous indifference" to individual rights, but held that its hands were tied. The U.S. Supreme Court declined to review the case on appeal, leaving the state police free to carry on as usual. The ugly issue would not go away, however.

In many ways, the 1970s was a time for new social movements. After a century of struggle, the civil rights revolution made major strides toward racial justice for African-Americans. Now other groups stepped forward to try to improve their standing — women, gays, students, the poor, the physically and developmentally disabled, prisoners and institutionalized people, Latinos and Native Americans. Some succeeded, others were forced to wait. But none scored more gains than the women's rights movement.

The ACLU had created a Women's Rights Project under the direction of Columbia law professor Ruth Bader Ginsburg in 1972. Within two years the ACLU, along with state affiliates, had entered more than 300 sex discrimination cases. The national office encouraged the affiliates to take an activist approach, but New Jersey hardly needed prodding. It already had a strong record of bringing sex discrimination claims. In fact, Ginsburg had handled some of them herself while teaching at Rutgers.

The ACLU-NJ took an early lead on abortion rights as well. In 1967 — well before states began liberalizing their criminal abortion laws, and six years before *Roe v. Wade* — its board of trustees voted to adopt a written position endorsing a woman's right to abortion. "The state should remain silent on the subject of abortion. The desire of the mother and the willingness of the physician, alone, shall govern the use of the several medical procedures collectively referred to as abortion," it said.

Three years later the ACLU-NJ successfully challenged New Jersey's 123-year-old abortion law, which made performing abortions "without lawful justification" a high misdemeanor. Until then state courts generally held that abortion was illegal except when performed to save a woman's life. The plaintiffs in *YWCA v. Kugler* included nine physicians (two of whom had lost their medical licenses), three women and a representative of the YWCA of Princeton, which had a committee on abortion reform. George Kugler was the state Attorney General.

A panel of federal judges overturned the law as unconstitutionally vague and an invasion of a woman's privacy, but declined to enjoin the state from enforcing the statute. That left doctors in a murky place, legally. Kugler announced he was appealing the decision, and emphasized that performing an abortion was still illegal. The ACLU-NJ came up with an immediate response:

It would defend any woman seeking an abortion, or any doctor threatened with prosecution.

A test case was not long in coming. Robert M. Livingston, an outspoken physician from Englewood Cliffs, was indicted by a Bergen County grand jury for conspiracy to perform an abortion. True to its word, the ACLU-NJ defended him. But there was no need for a trial. The U.S. Supreme Court, in *Roe v. Wade*, ruled that states had no right to interfere in an abortion during the first 12 weeks of pregnancy. Livingston's indictment was tossed out.

Some of the ACLU-NJ's best-known fights for gender equality were staged in the arena of high school sports. In 1972 the affiliate sued the New Jersey Interscholastic Athletic Association over a provision banning girls from participation in non-contact sports. "No girl may be permitted to participate in inter-scholastic athletic association contests in competition with boys," the rule said. Fifteen-year-old Abbe Seldin, a student at Teaneck High School who wanted to play with the boys varsity tennis team, was the plaintiff in the case.

Seldin, who went on to play professional tennis, had been serious about the game since turning 11. She was ranked No. 22 among

Teaneck High School student Abbe Seldin, who later played professional tennis, went to federal court in 1972 to win the right to join Teaneck's boys tennis team, as the school had no girls team. (Abbe Seldin)

15- and 16-year-olds by the Eastern Lawn Tennis Association. School officials said they were sympathetic to her desire to play on the varsity tennis team, but refused to let her try out. The lawsuit, brought by Rutgers law professor Annamay Sheppard and Ruth Bader Ginsburg, named state education officials as well as Teaneck school administrators. Because the state officials allowed the association to enforce the ban, the complaint stated, they were violating the equal protection guarantee of the U.S. Constitution. During the trial, U.S. District Court Judge Leonard I. Garth said he wanted to settle the dispute in a different venue — on the tennis court. "I would rather resolve this case by refereeing a match between Abbe and the top player from the men's team," Garth said. "I am perfectly willing to spend a couple of hours on the tennis court to save several days in my own court. I'll do anything to dispose of this case. I'll take her on myself if I have to." Garth didn't have to. During the trial, the association relaxed its rules to permit girls to participate in some sports. But the fight for gender equality in sports wasn't over.

Two years later the ACLU-NJ sued the interscholastic athletic association again. This time the plaintiff was Karen Christiano, a female fencer from Parsippany-Troy Hills. Christiano had played for the school's varsity fencing team two years earlier, but was dropped along with five other girls when the interscholastic association reclassified fencing as a contact sport. This time, the mere threat of a lawsuit prompted the association to act. Five days before the case was scheduled for trial, its executive board voted to revoke all discriminatory regulations.

Other civil actions alleging gender discrimination during this period covered a wide range of issues. The ACLU-NJ represented a woman whose auto insurance company cancelled her policy because she was living with a man "without benefit of wedlock;" a National Guardswoman discharged from her unit because she was an "unwed mother;" and a group of divorced women whose banks refused to give them loans unless their ex-husbands co-signed the loan agreements.

The prisoners' rights movement was another important off-shoot of the civil rights movement. During the late 1960s, a series of court rulings established that prisoners were entitled to Constitutional guarantees. An avalanche of prison litigation followed. Bloody prison uprisings in Attica, N.Y., and Rahway, N.J., in 1971 stirred interest in prison reform. The ACLU created a National Prison Project in Washington, D.C., the following year.

The New Jersey affiliate was actually ahead of the trend, having started a prisoners' rights project even before the uprisings, according to Lennox Hinds, a New Jersey attorney who started the project as a third-year law student at Rutgers. Hinds was older than most of his peers, and a seasoned community organizer, having worked as an organizer for the Congress of Racial Equality. The new project was called the Prisoner Rights Organized Defense, or PROD. By the time of the uprising at Rahway State Prison, Hinds knew some of the inmates. Some asked to see him after the rebellion began. "It was exciting, but there were a lot of disgruntled people around. I remember correctional officers saying, 'We can't guarantee your life.' I had a level of apprehension going in," he said.

The uprising at the maximum-security prison in Woodbridge on Thanksgiving Day, 1971, threw PROD into high gear. Unlike at Attica, where 39 people died, the Rahway revolt ended without any loss of life. Inmates took the prison warden and five guards hostage, but released them after negotiating an agreement with then-Gov. William Cahill to review a list of grievances. The inmates personally addressed the people of New Jersey in a petition airing their grievances. "We are desperately asking that you help us to obtain the right to exist as human beings," they wrote. Their list included demands for better food and medicine, religious freedom, improved vocational and educational training and tougher discipline for guards.

When the crisis ended, Cahill promised brutality and "corporal punishment" would not be tolerated as retribution for the uprising.

But one week later he called a press conference to announce that any inmate found to have committed a crime or violated prison rules would face criminal prosecution or institutional discipline. Several guards were stabbed during the revolt, and part of the prison was set on fire. Forty-one inmates were eventually indicted.

PROD brought its first riot-related lawsuit within days of the uprising. The suit, filed in federal court, alleged that prison officials hustled 24 supposed ringleaders out of Rahway as soon as the riot ended, transferred them to psychiatric units in other prisons, and wrote them up on unsubstantiated charges. The transfer was a violation of the inmates' right to due process, according to the complaint. One month later, PROD filed a second lawsuit. This one accused officials at Trenton State Prison of punishing four inmates for inciting a work stoppage.

During its nine years of existence PROD produced a heap of litigation. In one key case, Steve Latimer, a volunteer attorney, challenged the constitutionality of the notorious "Management Control Unit" of Trenton State Prison. The unit had 5-by-7-foot cells used for long-term isolation of inmates considered troublemakers. "The standard back then for an Eighth Amendment violation (cruel and unusual punishment) was, Did the conduct of the prison 'shock the conscience'? Those were the magic words," Latimer later recalled. "What the judge said, in that case, which we lost, is something I will never forget. He said, 'The conditions in this place shock my conscience, but not the judicial conscience.' I never understood how the judge separated himself the judge from himself the human being."

Few PROD lawsuits got extensive coverage in the press. One exception was a lawsuit filed on behalf of the estate of Daniel Hogan, a troubled 21-year-old from Union County scalded to death in a decrepit basement cell at Trenton State Prison on Dec. 27, 1973. The circumstances were horrifying. The cell, built before the Civil War, had been condemned as unfit for human habitation, but was considered appropriate for Hogan, who was awaiting psychiatric evaluation. One reached the cell by open-

Eric Neisser

Eric Neisser understood pain and loss from an early age. As a child, Neisser listened to his mother describe her escape from Austria during the Holocaust and learned the stories of his family members who perished. When he was 16, Neisser's older brother committed suicide.

"Those experiences gave him a deep sense of pain in the world," said his widow, Joan. "It made him want to make it a better place."

And that he did. Always energetic and upbeat, he devoted his legal career to fighting for civil rights, both in New Jersey and nationwide.

He volunteered as a cooperating attorney for the ACLU-NJ for years before serving as the organization's legal director. In a landmark case that tested the boundaries of the Fourth Amendment, Neisser and colleague Frank Askin helped convince the U.S. Supreme Court in 1979 that police must have a reasonable suspicion to stop a motorist for questioning. Neisser also became involved in one of the state's most bitterly contested murder cases, which went to the U.S. Supreme Court.

By the time Neisser left New Jersey to head the Franklin Pierce Law Center in New Hampshire, he had taught at Rutgers School of Law-Newark for 20 years, helping run the school's Constitutional Litigation Clinic and having at one point assumed the role of acting dean. The public interest law program at the law school was named in his honor. Neisser also founded the Special Education Clinic for disabled children.

ing a thick wooden door that had a small opening at the bottom, originally used to slide food inside. Beyond that locked door was a door with bars, then a step down into the cement cell. There was a drain in the cement floor.

On the day Hogan died, a pipe burst somewhere, this floor drain became clogged, and water began pouring from Hogan's toilet. The water rose in the cell and came into contact with radiator pipes, which heated the water to nearly boiling. As the night wore on, according to affidavits filed in the case, prisoners reportedly heard Hogan yell, "Help, Help, Help! I can't breathe! They are killing me! Let me out of here! I am burning up! Oh Lord I'm dying!" Guards were heard to respond, "I'm not coming," "Be quiet," and "Shut the fuck up!" When one guard did respond he observed a cloud of steam, but told Hogan he couldn't help and slammed the door. As the hours passed, the cries became feebler and eventually stopped altogether. Early the next morning Hogan was found dead, floating face down in 9½ inches of steaming water. His body was covered with first-, second- and third-degree burns.

Leora Mosston, Hinds' successor at PROD, filed a wrongful-death suit seeking $1 million in damages. Mosston was in her 30s, with three children, but fresh out of law school. Hogan's grieving mother, a sad, dejected figure, reminded her of the "drained women that I grew up with, in the Irish neighborhoods" of the Highbridge section of the Bronx, N.Y. Asked to recall the case nearly 40 years later, Mosston described a meeting with an arrogant deputy attorney general who "just couldn't believe that anyone would dare sue the state for such a thing." Yet the facts were not in dispute, and the state settled for $30,000. No one was prosecuted criminally.

To this day Mosston believes her case got attention only because Hogan was white. "I am quite sure that, had he been black, there would not have been so much interest," she said. "It was a horrible case, but many horrible things happened at Trenton State Prison. It was a racist, callous, indifferent place."

Around this time ACLU-NJ executive director Stephen Nagler began looking for ways to finance another ambitious project. In a request for funding he dubbed it "New Jersey's Harvest of Shame." "South Jersey is one of the country's worst areas for migrant workers. Their poverty and despair will not change until they are brought under the full protection of constitutional guarantees," Nagler wrote. "An office in Bridgeton staffed by a full-time lawyer is needed."

Thousands of Puerto Ricans picked crops on New Jersey vegetable farms under a contract between the Commonwealth of Puerto Rico and the Glassboro Service Association, a nonprofit group of about 250 farmers associated with the New Jersey Farm Bureau. Any farmer needing labor called the association, which would transport workers from its barracks in Glassboro. The arrangement dated back to 1947.

South Jersey farmers had a well-deserved reputation for hostility toward outsiders. Many of their field hands lived in squalid conditions, in housing that looked more like chicken coops than housing for humans. For many years the farmers had been able to use a state trespass law to keep interested parties off their property; in 1970 a farmer in Cumberland County managed to get a lawyer and caseworker from Camden County Legal Services, Inc. arrested when they tried to inspect his property. One year later, in a case in which the ACLU-NJ participated, the New Jersey Supreme Court ruled that farmers could no longer invoke the trespass law to keep out legitimate visitors. The farmers turned to threats and intimidation to shield the camps from scrutiny.

A famous incident occurred in 1974, when a farmer physically attacked Byron Baer, a New Jersey assemblyman from Bergen County interested in sponsoring legislation to improve migrant labor conditions. Baer had arrived unannounced at a camp in Swedesboro with a small group in tow, including a reporter for The

Star-Ledger of Newark. The farmer and his foreman picked up boards and charged the group. Baer ended up with a broken arm, and the others left bruised and shaken. No one was convicted in the attack. Baer took another farm tour the following summer. This time, he was allowed to inspect the facilities at will. He called the housing unfit for humans and criticized the federal government for failing to enforce standards. Responsibility had shifted from the state to the U.S. Occupational Safety and Health Administration.

Nagler was awarded grants from two foundations to finance the new program, established in 1975 as the Farmworkers Rights Project. To run it he recruited a dynamic young lawyer, Michael Berger, who had litigated many contract disputes between farmers and workers while director of the farmworker division of Camden Regional Legal Services. The project opened in a storefront office on High Street in Glassboro, not far from the Glassboro Service Association.

As a Legal Services lawyer, Berger had sued individual farmers in the state courts. Now he scouted for civil liberties violations affecting a group or entire class of workers. He did not have to look far. "The housing was deplorable, and living conditions were ridiculous and difficult. The crew leaders would sell food and beverages and liquor to the workers at inflated prices, and then withhold wages for repayment," Berger said years later. "The farmworkers worked long, long hours, and were not taking home any money. There were physical abuses, crime and punishing working conditions."

The Farmworkers Rights Project sued the Glassboro Service Association over numerous issues, including pay, housing and the right to organize. It also brought civil actions against the state. One sought to compel enforcement of sanitation laws requiring running water and toilets; another challenged a provision of state law that denied farm workers overtime pay. New Jersey required workers to be paid time and a half for time put in over 40 hours, but exempted farm workers. They were paid minimum wage, no matter how long they worked. Most of the time, it was 15 hours a

In 1975, the ACLU-NJ established the Farmworkers Rights Project, providing much-needed legal services to farmworkers whose rights to organize were trampled. (New Jersey State Archives, Department of State)

day, seven days a week. Berger also won an important case in New Jersey Supreme Court, barring farm owners from evicting workers without a court order.

The Farmworkers Rights Project continued to provide free legal assistance to workers through the 1980s. Angel Dominguez, who directed the program after 1980, was instrumental in helping farmworkers organize a union, el Comite Organizador de Trabajadores Agricolas (COTA). During the peach harvest in 1980, 50 farm workers organized and went on strike, for the first time ever, after a farmer refused to meet their demand to raise pay over the state minimum wage. Today the Farmworkers Rights Project lives on as the Farmworkers Support Committee in Bridgeton, also known as El Comité de Apoyo a los Trabajadores Agricolas (CATA).

In the winter of 1973 a 15-year-old New Jersey student named Lori Paton became embroiled in a free-speech controversy that ended up clouding five years of her life. It began with a homework assignment for one of her classes at West Morris-Mendham High School, a social studies course called "Left to Right." The assignment required students to write letters to various political organizations requesting information about their political philosophy. Paton decided to write to the Socialist Labor Party in New York City, then on its last legs, but inadvertently wrote the address of the Socialist Workers Party, an active anti-war group. It sent her a newspaper and some printed material. Her letter, meanwhile, touched off an immediate FBI investigation of Paton, her family and her teacher. The resulting notoriety, which included an article in the school newspaper about her being under investigation by the FBI, upset Paton. She also worried it could have an impact on a future career.

At the time, the Socialist Workers Party was the target of a "mail cover," an investigative technique used against people or groups engaged in criminal activity, having fugitive status, or considered subversive. Postal clerks did not open incoming letters to targets of mail covers, but did record everything on the outside of the envelope. A postal clerk sent Lori Paton's home address in Chester Township to the FBI, which checked to see if her name came up in its files. It didn't. An FBI agent drove to Chester and visited the chief of police, who told him none of the Paton family had a criminal record. He went to her high school, where the principal explained the genesis of the letter. Then the agent wrote a memo suggesting the case be closed. Nonetheless, a card bearing the teenager's name was entered into a master file in Washington with the notation "S.M.-S.W.P.", or "Subversive Material-Socialist Workers Party."

Paton's teacher urged her to go to the ACLU-NJ, which filed a federal lawsuit on her behalf. The FBI initially denied they had investigated Paton, something she resented. While testifying years later in Washington, D.C., during a hearing on privacy concerns, Paton said: "I was initially surprised to find that I had been the subject of an FBI investigation, but I found it even more incredible that a representative of my government would lie to me in this way."

Early on in the case a judge ordered the FBI to destroy her file, but he denied her claim that mail covers were an unconstitutional abuse of police power. In 1978, however, a judge in federal District Court in Newark ruled that it was unconstitutional for investigative agencies to scrutinize citizens' mail in the name of "national security."

In 1979 the ACLU-NJ enjoyed a satisfying victory in a Delaware case involving random police stops. A Delaware police officer admitted stopping a car to ask for the driver's license and registration because he had nothing else to do. While walking toward the car he spotted a bag of marijuana on the floor, and arrested the driver. Nearly 10 years earlier the affiliate had moved against the New Jersey State Police in a similar case, only to see its work aborted by a U.S. Supreme Court decision. Now public defenders in Delaware were about to fight for a state court ruling before the high court, and asked the ACLU-NJ to be co-counsel because volunteer attorney Frank Askin had spent so many years laying out arguments in similar cases that he was an expert on the subject. His lawyers argued the evidence should be thrown out because the stop violated the Fourth Amendment guarantee against unreasonable search and seizure.

The Supreme Court agreed, with only Associate Justice William Rehnquist dissenting. Police could not constitutionally stop a driver without having "articulable and reasonable suspicion" that some violation of law had occurred. "Were the individual subject to unfettered government intrusion every time he entered an automobile, the security guaranteed by the Fourth Amendment would be seriously circumscribed," the court held.

Askin was pleasantly surprised by the decision. He predicted, however, that it might lead police to invent reasons for suspicion. In a memoir published much later, Askin said state police pulled him over about six months after the Delaware decision.

"I am not sure whether he had 'articulable suspicion' that I was violating some traffic law — but any cop with half a brain can always articulate a legitimate reason for a highway stop. Anyway, this officer discovered that I was a law professor and asked me what I thought 'of the recent decision that we can't stop you without reason.' It was a deserted country road, and I wasn't about to confess my involvement in the case," Askin wrote. "I merely said, 'Oh, I didn't think that was such a bad decision.' He responded, 'I ought to give you a ticket for that.' But he didn't."

CHAPTER FOUR

Assaults on the Bill of Rights

One Teacher Risks His Career

Physics teacher Jeff May risked his career in 1982 when he defied a state law requiring public schools to start the day with a moment of silence. (Ed Hill/northjersey.com)

Jeff May went to Syracuse University figuring he'd major in physics. He did, but realized after a couple years' study that what he wanted was to teach the subject.

Once he got his bachelor's degree, he took graduate courses to get his teaching certification. By 1982 he was comfortably ensconced as a physics teacher at John P. Stevens High School in Edison Township. May was 36 years old, with 14 years experience. After a number of years instructing ninth-grade science, he was finally teaching the subject he loved.

Then he risked everything.

On Dec. 22, 1982, the first day of a new law requiring public schools to start the day with a moment of silence, May committed an act of civil disobedience. Instead of enforcing 60 seconds of silence in homeroom, he opened his mouth and talked. First, he took roll. When that failed to take up the full minute, he talked some more. In so doing, he became the only public school teacher in New Jersey to defy the will of the state Legislature that students begin each day with a minute of silence for "quiet and private contemplation or introspection."

Being a respectful sort of person, May had stopped by his principal's office earlier that morning to let him know of his plan. He even brought along a card on which he had listed his objections to the law, the main ones being that it was unconstitutional and went against his conscience. "It was just not part of my job description to throw a religious-type ceremony at the beginning of every day," May recalled years later. "My philosophy was to lead students outward, not inward. It was contrary to everything I thought education was about. The principal said, 'Well, Jeff, I understand, but I have to do what I have to do.' During homeroom he stood outside my door, which I always left open. The announcement came: 'We are now going to have a moment of silence.' I talked through the whole thing. The students were like, 'Mr. May, Mr. May, you're supposed to be quiet!' "

May believed that the legislature's intention was to foster school prayer. At one time New Jersey schools required Bible readings (and permitted the Lord's Prayer) during opening exercises, but abandoned the practice after the U.S. Supreme Court, in a New York case, declared school-sponsored prayer unconstitutional in 1962. The New Jersey legislature subsequently passed at least a dozen bills to re-introduce prayer, but three different governors vetoed them as unnecessary or unconstitutional.

In 1982, determined legislators took a new approach, passing a bill requiring a "moment of silence." The bill did not mention prayer, and stated the moment was "to be used solely at the discretion of the individual student." Gov. Thomas H. Kean vetoed it anyway. The legislature overrode his veto, and the bill became law. Saul Cooperman, the state's Education Commissioner, immediately issued a directive advising school districts.

One of May's homeroom students tipped off a local newspaper about his defiance of the law. It ran a story without revealing his name. Then the Associated Press picked up the story and identified May. Jeff Fogel, now the executive director of the American Civil Liberties Union of New Jersey, called May and asked if he wanted to be a plaintiff in a federal lawsuit, along with some parents and students. He agreed. The ACLU-NJ filed suit on their behalf in January 1983, seeking to overturn the law and temporarily halt implementation. District Court Judge Dickinson R. Debevoise issued an injunction and scheduled a trial.

May missed only one day of class that year, when he was called to the superintendent's office. His supervisor relieved him of homeroom duties, but did not interfere with his teaching. Everyone understood his job was on the line — if the judge upheld the law, he'd be fired — but life went on in the meantime. May worried, but didn't agonize, and certainly never regretted his decision. "I felt good about it," he said. "It wasn't fun. But it was something I had to do. There was really no choice." He discussed the issue with colleagues only if they inquired, and never brought it up with students. If a student asked, he ignored the question. May believed his job was to teach physics, not talk about personal feelings or try to influence students. A newspaper reporter, curious about May, attempted a personality profile. He answered her questions, but revealed very little. He described himself as an agnostic. He said he went to high school in New Rochelle, N.Y., and graduated from Syracuse, but declined to discuss his personal life. Asked if he had any heroes, he named Ralph Nader and Albert Einstein.

The decision came down on Oct. 24, 1983. Judge Debevoise ruled that the moment of silence violated the First Amendment and was an "obvious attempt to cross the forbidden line" separating church and state. "The State has injected itself into religious matters by designating a time and place when children and teachers may pray . . . and by mandating conduct by all other children and teachers so that the prayers may proceed uninterrupted in their presence," he said.

The legislature's two leaders appealed the decision, but lost. Undeterred, they appealed to the U.S. Supreme Court. The high court refused to reinstate the law on procedural grounds, saying the two men no longer held leadership positions in the legislature and lacked standing to sue. It was December 1987, five years after May's act of civil disobedience. For the plaintiffs, there was no victory party. A colleague or two came up to May at school to extend congratulations, but most seemed to have forgotten about the case. His career didn't suffer, at least not permanently. School officials sent May back to teach in junior high in 1984, but the assignment lasted only a year.

"Maybe it was retribution, I don't know, but eventually they needed a physics teacher at J.P. Stevens. Everyone knew I was highly qualified," he reflected. He taught in the district for many years, and retired in 2009.

May v. Cooperman was a huge win for the ACLU-NJ, and had been a risk for the organization. Some 25 states had adopted moment-of-silence laws, including New York and Connecticut, and none had been challenged. Not everyone was in favor of the ACLU-NJ suing. "There was a person on the national ACLU legal staff who thought we were crazy to take it on," Fogel said. "He said a moment of silence wasn't necessarily prayer. I remember telling him, 'You're not sitting here in New Jersey. All the legislators are saying it is about prayer.'"

When Fogel took over as executive director in 1982, it was a homecoming of sorts. He had been associated with the affiliate off and on since law school. Prior to taking the position, he had specialized in civil rights litigation as staff counsel for the Puerto Rican Law Project in San Juan. In an interview shortly after his return to Newark, he complained about the state of the state, and the spirit of the times. The 1970s had been a progressive and exhilarating decade for civil rights activists. Now the Bill of Rights was undergoing "massive assaults," he said. The ACLU needed to stiffen its spine.

Ronald Reagan, who had campaigned "to make America great again," was in the second year of his eight-year-long presidency. His wife, Nancy, had begun the "Just Say No" campaign against drugs. The Rev. Jerry Falwell of the Moral Majority, a political action group of conservative Christians he founded in 1979, advocated a return to "family values," and condemned abortion and homosexuality. Public anxiety was mounting over AIDS, which did not yet have a name. Anti-abortion networks committing to overturning *Roe v. Wade* were forming in many parts of the country. On the other hand, family life in the U.S. continued its transformation, churning out more divorce, more single parents, and more unmarried people living together than ever. Gender roles were blurring. Feminists were still advocating for equality, yet women were also starting to achieve big "firsts." Sandra Day O'Connor had just become the first woman to serve on the U.S. Supreme Court.

Conflict between progressive and conservative forces caused backlash in New Jersey, too. Two special ACLU-NJ projects from earlier decades — CLAW, the civil liberties storefront in Newark, and PROD, the prisoner rights defense group — lost funding and faded away, but a Women's Rights Project started in Trenton. One of the new project's first tasks was to figure out how to expedite implementation of a recent New Jersey Supreme Court ruling on abortion funding for low-income women.

The case, litigated by Rutgers law professor Nadine Taub, overturned a state law prohibiting Medicaid-financed abortions except when necessary to save the mother's life. The ruling was an important victory for the ACLU-NJ, but as a practical matter many obstacles facing poor women remained. Hospitals were reluctant to provide the service, especially in South Jersey, and Medicaid reimbursement levels were very low. The Women's Rights Project lobbied for the state to make needed changes.

During the 1980s the ACLU-NJ participated in a multitude of cases on behalf of women. One challenged the constitutionality of excluding women from serving as foremen of grand juries. Another took on the New Jersey Department of Personnel, arguing a physical performance test was discriminatory, applied arbitrary standards, and was unrelated to a police officer's ability to do the job. The ACLU-NJ filed the suit on behalf of female officers who failed a physical performance test. (The state settled the case in 1994 and set up a fund for victims.) A third noteworthy case helped establish that expert testimony about "battered woman syndrome" was admissible as evidence in murder cases. The ruling, issued by the New Jersey Supreme Court in 1984, arose from an Essex County criminal case dating back to 1980. Gladys Kelly of East Orange fatally stabbed her husband with a pair of scissors. At trial Kelly did not deny the stabbing, but testified she acted in self-defense after years of beatings. An expert testified about the effects of battered woman syndrome, but the trial court excluded the testimony. The Supreme Court ordered the case re-tried.

Not every challenge succeeded. In 1986, a federal appeals court ruled that Kiwanis International could exclude women. The case developed after the Kiwanis Club of Ridgewood defied national bylaws by extending membership to a local woman. Kiwanis International, its parent organization, struck back by revoking the club's charter. A lower court ruled that Kiwanis International violated the New Jersey Law Against Discrimination, but the appeals court reversed. Kiwanis was a selective private club, not a public accommodation, and was entitled to bar women. In the end, the organization voted to go co-ed in 1987, following in the footsteps of the Jaycees and Lions International.

Beth Balsley was beaten up by her teammates after she won her right in court to join the North Hunterdon football team in 1985. (Star-Ledger photographs © The Star-Ledger, Newark, NJ)

Of the many gender discrimination claims brought by the ACLU-NJ during the decade, two stand out. Both involved young women with true grit.

The first was Beth Balsley, a 127-pound junior at North Hunterdon High School who was determined to play football. For this she was shunned, terrorized, and beaten up by her own teammates. The second was Sally Frank, who spent 13 years battling the hidebound traditions and well-financed opposition of the all-male eating clubs at Princeton University, her alma mater. She, too, was harassed for daring to challenge the existing order. Frank's long fight started when she was an undergraduate. By the time it was over, she was a law professor.

Beth Balsley's football career actually started with lacrosse. In the spring of her sophomore year at high school, she tried out for the lacrosse team. Only boys played on the team, but she didn't care. She had two older brothers, who included her in their games while she was growing up. Balsley loved lacrosse, but her coaches cut her. That's when she decided to go out for football, which had a no-cuts policy. Anyone who tried out for football at North Hunterdon was allowed to practice with the team. "Part of it was, I believed in equality. I didn't like that whole perception about a girl being the weaker sex. And part was that I wanted to play a contact collision sport. I just wanted a physical way to get out my aggression," she said years afterward.

No one, however, wanted her on the team — not the football coaches, nor the athletic director, nor the board of education. Balsley circulated a petition and presented it at a school board meeting. Edison Township physics teacher Jeff May — still a plaintiff in the pending moment-of-silence case — read an article about her efforts and called to offer support. When he learned she had no advocates — her parents approved, but only from the sidelines, and they were not about to hire a lawyer — he suggested she contact the ACLU-NJ.

The affiliate filed a petition with the New Jersey Commissioner of Education, arguing that excluding Balsley from the team violated education and civil rights laws. An administrative law judge agreed, and ordered school authorities to grant Balsley's request. She suited up for the junior varsity team, and became the first girl in New Jersey to be allowed to participate in a boys contact sport.

Balsley tried out as defensive back, but was made a nose tackle. She played in one game, on Oct. 21, 1985, with media from all over metropolitan New York watching. A substitute coach sent her in during the third quarter, when her team was up 17-0. During the next six plays, she took a brutal beating. "I'm the worst player on the team, but the boys have had more years at this," she told The New York Times. "I swear I'll give it everything I have to catch up."

Her pluck did not win her many admirers. At school, pretty much everyone ostracized her. Nevertheless, during her senior year, she never missed a practice. One day a coach warned her not

Maggie McCool

Maggie McCool expected some resistance when she told her 10th-grade biology teacher she would not dissect worms, frogs or fetal pigs because of her religious beliefs.

Administrators at Woodstown High School were known for disciplining students who questioned their authority. But McCool never imagined the school would flunk her for refusing to take a knife to the animals.

"I thought of myself as a very peaceful person and thought I could settle it through persuasion," she said.

She thought wrong. When the district refused to change her grades, McCool's father, a lifelong member of the ACLU, sought help from the New Jersey affiliate to sue the district for violating her freedom of religion. While McCool was not a member of any religious body, she held a deep religious conviction about the sanctity of life.

Just before the case was to go to trial on July 24, 1989, the Woodstown-Pilesgrove Board of Education agreed to settle the case and recalculated her grades.

McCool became a teacher in Delaware, working with students who have emotional and behavioral disabilities. Her case made her more sensitive to the beliefs of her own students.

"It has impacted how I look at other individuals," she said.

to go to practice after school. When she asked why, he said, "You're going to get beat up." "What else is new?" she said, laughing. Later that afternoon she started to wonder what he had meant. She knew as soon as she reported for practice, when three teammates converged on her. "Can I at least put on my helmet?" she asked. They punched her and threw her to the ground. Other players formed a tight circle around them. "They hit me with tackling dummies, I was bleeding on the gravel. Nobody stood up to help me. I thought, 'I can quit, or I can show them this is not how you get what you want.' And I kept going to practice."

After high school, Balsley was seriously injured in a car accident. At the end of her rehabilitation, doctors said her brain had suffered lasting damage, that she could not return to college. Balsley was shattered, but her mother reminded her she had heard something similar before. "The coaches told you you couldn't play football, and look what you did. These people don't know what you're capable of."

Balsley went back to college, where she managed the football team, and graduated. Then she went to graduate school, and earned a master's degree in social work. She married. Today she works with people with chronic mental health issues. "I try to help them with things society has told them they can't do," said Balsley, now Beth Gross. "I encourage them to move forward and pursue their dreams. I'm 41 years old, but I still don't like people in authority telling others what they can or can't do."

Sally Frank's story starts in her first year of college, when she tried to join one of Princeton's selective males-only eating clubs. It was an audacious move. Frank was rebuffed, but tried again the following year.

The eating clubs selected new members through a process called "bicker," in which students applied for membership and members bid, or "bickered," for new members. In the fall of

Sally Frank celebrates after a protracted court battle forced Princeton University's all-male eating clubs to admit women in 1992. (The Associated Press)

1978, Frank, now 19 and a sophomore, decided to attend a pre-bicker party at one of the clubs. "The party allowed members to get to know folks who wanted to bicker," she recalled more than 30 years later. "I expected conversation repartee. Beer was flowing downstairs. I was upstairs, talking to one of the members of the club."

The first sign of trouble came when someone poured a beer over Frank's head from behind. A second followed, landing just behind her head. "Then 20 to 30 guys came from downstairs, where they'd been drinking. They threatened to throw me in the fountain."

Shaken, Frank left and returned to her dorm room. She locked the door. Around 2 a.m., she heard someone run through the hall. Then a male voice said, "Her door is locked." When it was quiet again, Frank left and spent the night with friends. Ultimately Frank filed a sex discrimination complaint against three eating clubs — Ivy Club, Tiger Inn and Cottage Club — with the New Jersey Division of Civil Rights. She also named Princeton University in the complaint, contending that the university supported the clubs in various ways.

The eating clubs, stately presences along Princeton's Prospect Avenue, had existed since 1879 and served as the social center for upperclass life. All had an elaborate selective admissions process. When the university began admitting women in 1969, the

Madhavi Sunder

When she started as editor in chief of Mainland Regional High School's student newspaper in the late 1980s, Madhavi Sunder didn't know much about the American Civil Liberties Union. But by the time her term on Hoofprints was over, she was grateful to the ACLU for protecting her from a false accusation of libel.

An article in Hoofprints about possible steroid use by student athletes — and about a possible source of the supplements found within the local Gold's Gym — caught the attention of the fitness club's owner. He took umbrage and sued, alleging libel. In 1989, Frank Corrado took on the case, which would become his first with the organization.

During depositions, the high school football coach admitted he had told the team to stay away from Gold's, fearing they would be tempted to use the steroids he suspected were available there. Upon hearing his sworn statement, the gym's owners dismissed the lawsuit against Sunder in 1990, who was by then an undergraduate at Harvard University.

"The ACLU showed me that the promise of freedom in America is not merely theoretical," says Sunder.

The experience inspired Sunder's career choice: she went on to Stanford Law School and became a professor of law at the University of California, Davis, focusing on the primacy of dissent in a democracy. She has been a visiting professor at Yale Law School, the University of Chicago Law School and Cornell Law School.

clubs had to decide whether to accept female classmates. Most did, with the exception of Ivy, Tiger Inn and Cottage. At the time Frank was initially denied admission, she was volunteering for the ACLU-NJ. One of the lawyers there encouraged her to sue, saying he believed the clubs functioned as public accommodations and were violating New Jersey's law against discrimination. The clubs, which owned their own land and buildings, had always considered themselves private institutions.

In 1979, Frank filed a complaint with the state Division on Civil Rights, which held the clubs were private and declined to investigate. When Frank persisted the agency relented and investigated, but dismissed her claim. Frank appealed to the courts, which ordered the division to investigate further. The graduate president of Ivy was miffed, but attempted a joke. "We've taken every form of mankind except womankind, and they're welcome at meals and at parties," he told The New York Times.

After sifting through a record consisting of thousands of pages, the civil rights agency finally ordered a hearing. It was 1984, five years after Frank filed her complaint. Frank was now a lawyer herself, having graduated from New York University School of Law the previous year. In the meantime, Nadine Taub, director of the Women's Rights Litigation Clinic at Rutgers School of Law, had joined Frank as her co-counsel.

An administrative judge ruled in favor of Frank in 1985. One of the clubs, Cottage, settled in 1986, as did Princeton University; Cottage paid Frank damages and agreed to admit female members. Ivy and Tiger Inn resisted, however, beginning a fresh battle.

Eventually the issue came before the New Jersey Supreme Court, which ruled that the last two clubs were public accommodations and ordered them to admit women. Frank, a 1980 Princeton grad, had just attended her 10th class reunion. Further appeals kept the case alive until the U.S. Supreme Court refused to review the case in 1991. Ivy and Tiger Inn had to pay the ACLU $43,000 in legal fees.

Today Sally Frank is a professor of law at Drake University in
Des Moines, Iowa, and an attorney in private practice. She has
represented many activists involved in civil disobedience.

The first AIDS-like illnesses were reported in the U.S. in
1978, but the disease was not recognized as a new clinical syndrome until 1981. After that the cases started piling up, especially
in California and New York. In fall 1981 the federal Center for
Disease Control and Prevention documented 100 cases; within
little more than a year, the number stood at 3,000. By the mid-
1980s, New Jersey was reporting HIV infections in large numbers of women and minorities. The general population reacted
with paranoia and fear.

In 1987, the ACLU-NJ was responsible for one of the first
reported legal challenges to discrimination based on HIV/AIDS.
A Jersey City landlord refused to rent an apartment to three gay
men on the grounds that they could get AIDS and spread it to his
family, who lived in the same building. The case established that
AIDS was a disability under the state's anti-discrimination law
and that people with HIV/AIDS — including those who were
perceived to have it — were entitled to legal protection. Even so,
AIDS discrimination cases multiplied. The ACLU-NJ intervened when a private elementary school kicked out a child on
scholarship whose siblings were HIV-positive. The ACLU-NJ
also took a dentist to federal court for refusing to take care of
an HIV-positive patient who had cracked his tooth in an auto
accident. It charged the Camden County dentist with violating the New Jersey Law Against Discrimination and the federal
Americans with Disabilities Act — and won. The judge ruled that
the dentist's clinic was a public accommodation, and awarded the
patient $50,000 in damages. By that time, however, the dentist
had vanished.

Beginning around 1980, the ACLU-NJ began to receive numerous complaints about unreasonable searches of students by school officials. The Fourth Amendment to the Constitution provides a guarantee against unreasonable search and seizure, but many school administrators believed they had the authority to search students and their possessions. The ACLU-NJ took the position that school officials searching a student must adhere to the same standards of probable cause as any other governmental agent, and argued that evidence produced in illegal searches should be excluded from criminal or judicial proceedings.

One of the most important cases on students' constitutional rights during this era came out of Piscataway Township. It started in 1980 when an assistant principal searched a 14-year-old student reported for smoking in the girls' bathroom in violation of school rules. When the girl, identified in law books as "T.L.O.," denied having smoked, the assistant principal opened her purse. Seeing cigarettes and some rolling papers, he did a full search of the contents and found items — empty bags, some marijuana, a pipe — that suggested the student was using and dealing marijuana. The vice principal notified the student's mother and the police, who took the student to the police station. She admitted selling marijuana and was adjudicated delinquent in juvenile court. Later the student filed a lawsuit seeking to suppress the evidence seized during the search, on the grounds it violated the Fourth Amendment. The ACLU-NJ participated in the case, arguing that schools needed probable cause to search a student.

She lost. Although the New Jersey Supreme Court deemed the search illegal, the U.S. Supreme Court reversed, saying public school officials may search students if there is "reasonable suspicion" a law or school rule has been violated. Disappointed, the ACLU-NJ published a commentary in its newsletter saying it hoped the state constitution would do a better job of protecting students' rights in the future.

The opportunity was not long in coming. In August 1985 the Carlstadt-East Rutherford Regional School District adopted the extraordinary policy of requiring every one of the 516 students attending Henry P. Becton Regional High School to undergo blood and urine tests for drugs. Families of students were shocked; only 28 students at the school had been referred for drug counseling. Under the policy — believed to be unique in the country — any student who refused the test would be expelled from school. The district said it wanted only to rehabilitate students, not punish them, and promised the results would not be turned over to police.

The ACLU-NJ immediately challenged the policy in state court, on behalf of five Becton students and their parents. Their lawsuit contended that the tests violated federal and state prohibitions against unreasonable searches. A Superior Court judge upheld their claims, saying urine tests violated students' constitutional right to due process, as well as their right to privacy. "Defendants' policy is an attempt to control student discipline under the guise of a medical procedure," the judge ruled.

Students were not the only people being subjected to urine tests. All kinds of workers were finding themselves subject to random drug tests. ACLU-NJ lawyers intervened on behalf of employees of a number of police agencies, including the city of Plainfield, the Passaic County Sheriff's Office and the Newark Police Department's narcotics squad. In the Plainfield case, surprise urine tests administered to police and fire personnel netted 20 individuals who tested positive. When the city gave them a choice of resigning or facing charges, 17 sued in federal court. Their case, alleging an unconstitutional invasion of privacy, was successful. The victory did not last long. Today many public employees can be tested — but not all — depending on their type of employment.

ACLU-NJ legal director Eric Neisser and volunteer attorneys also participated in a notable lawsuit challenging mandatory drug testing at Coastal Eagle Point Oil in Westville, an oil refinery. The case started in 1986, when pumper James Hennessey was fired after a random test showed traces of marijuana and Valium in his urine. The worker won a victory in state Superior Court, but the appellate division upheld random testing by private employers. The New Jersey Supreme Court concurred, saying Hennessey had a "safety-sensitive" job in which drug-free performance was important. The job was dangerous, and the potential for deadly error — resulting in fire or explosion — high. "Although employees have a right to be protected from intrusions of privacy, we must also consider the competing public interest in safety," the court ruled.

Around 1987 a diligent staffer at the ACLU-NJ discerned a pattern to citizens' complaints about the New Jersey State Police. Callers who reported having been stopped and searched on the New Jersey Turnpike tended to be either minority males, or young drivers traveling alone in new cars — people fitting the stereotype of a drug courier. Troopers would typically claim the driver had some kind of problem, ask a lot of questions and search the car. If no contraband was found, they let them go without writing a ticket. ACLU-NJ office staff, under the stewardship of Legal Director Eric Neisser, decided to collect as much detail as possible about such stops.

The issue of profiling was not new. The ACLU-NJ's 1970 lawsuit alleging state police harassed long-haired travelers had been unsuccessful. This time, rather than go it alone, the ACLU-NJ formed a coalition with the NAACP, public defenders and interested volunteers. It organized a statewide conference about the problem. Intake staff instructed callers how to file grievances with the state police's Internal Affairs unit. The ACLU-NJ even conducted sensitivity training workshops for state police. Racial profiling got even more attention in 1989, when Joe Collum, an investigative reporter for Channel 9, produced a special report, "Without Just Cause," substantiating minorities' allegations. According to his analysis, minorities comprised five percent of Turnpike drivers — but represented nearly 80 percent of those arrested. In January 1990 Gov. Jim Florio appointed a new head of the state police, Col. Justin Dintino, who promised reforms. "I would rather see a drop in drug-related statistics than have troopers violating the rights of the driving public. Let the word go forth: There will be no activity that abridges the rights of any citizen," Dintino announced on his first day on the job. But the problem did not go away. The issue of racial profiling continued to bedevil New Jersey, and the ACLU-NJ, for years to come.

CHAPTER FIVE

Unease in the Age of Prosperity

Peace Activists Stake New Ground for Free Speech

In a case in which courts decided free speech trumped the rights of private property owners, the Rev. Bob Moore and the Coalition for Peace Action won the right in 1994 to leaflet in shopping malls. (Amanda Brown)

*I*t was November 1990, and the United States was on the brink of war with Iraq. Iraqi President Saddam Hussein had invaded and annexed Kuwait. President George H.W. Bush, backed by an international coalition of world powers, demanded he withdraw at once. When Hussein didn't budge, Bush deployed thousands of American troops into the Persian Gulf.

In Princeton, N.J., the Rev. Robert Moore of the Coalition for Peace Action was organizing a series of anti-war protests for the upcoming Veterans Day weekend. The coalition had printed 100,000 leaflets urging citizens to persuade their congressional representatives to vote against military intervention, and was planning to hand them out at 10 regional malls throughout New Jersey.

On Saturday, Nov. 10, Moore and seven fellow activists met at the Quakerbridge Mall in Lawrence Township. Once inside, they separated into four pairs and headed in different directions. After leafleting for about 30 minutes, Moore saw mall security approaching. "They told us we had to leave. We didn't. We explained what we were doing, and why. That's when they threatened us with arrest," he recalled.

Protesters leafleting at the other nine malls had the same experience, and it was no accident. One member of Moore's group was a lawyer with ties to the ACLU-NJ. During a strategy session he had suggested leafleting at malls. The lawyer knew malls prohibited leafleting, but believed the exercise would serve two goals. First, thousands of shoppers would be exposed to the group's message, at least until police intervened. Second, the ACLU-NJ — which had been trying to establish the right to leaflet in malls for years — would have the test case it needed.

While the anti-war protesters' efforts failed to stop the bombardment of Iraq, the test case succeeded. Four years later, in a 4-to-3 vote, the New Jersey Supreme Court ruled that shopping malls are de facto public forums and must allow access to people leafleting on social issues. The court interpreted the free-speech provisions of the state constitution as extending to malls, and decided free speech rights trumped the rights of private property owners.

"The economic lifeblood once found downtown has moved to the suburban shopping centers, which have substantially displaced the downtown business districts as the centers of commercial and social activity," the court said in the case, *New Jersey Coalition Against the War in the Middle East v. J.M.B. Realty.* "The flow of free speech in today's society is too important to be cut off simply to enhance the shopping ambience in our state's shopping centers."

The victory was especially sweet for Frank Askin, director of the Rutgers Constitutional Litigation Clinic, who litigated the case on behalf of the ACLU-NJ. In 1982 he had been refused permission to campaign at Livingston Mall while running for the Democratic

Congressional nomination in New Jersey's 11th District. Also, the mall case had been a tough case to win. The plaintiffs had lost in Superior Court and again in the Appellate Division.

For the Rev. Moore, the victory was not quite so sweet. Although the state Supreme Court had upheld his right to leaflet, it also said malls were entitled to promulgate "reasonable" regulations governing protesters' conduct. "After the decision we went right back to the Quakerbridge Mall, and found the rules to be quite restrictive. You could never have more than three people, you had to be within three feet of your assigned table, and the table, of course, was in the least busy part of the mall," he said.

Moore also found most shoppers didn't want to hear his message. "We had quite a few negative responses. People who go to malls are there to shop. The reality, we discovered, is that people are in commercial mode. They don't want to hear what we have to say. We consider it a moral and spiritual matter, of course, but they consider it a political message."

The shopping mall victory came in the middle of an unusual decade for New Jersey and the nation. The 1990s were a time of relative prosperity and peace. Technology was beginning to transform lives, through pager devices and the Internet. President Bill Clinton, who took office in 1993, was the dominant political figure. The country as a whole became increasingly sensitive to the rights of minorities and women, but social conservatives pushed back. University of Wyoming student Matthew Shepard, who was gay, was tortured and left to die one night in 1998, prompting state and federal legislators to pass hate crime legislation.

In New Jersey, Jim Florio, governor from 1990 until 1994, raised taxes to balance the budget and sent more money to poor school districts. Christine Todd Whitman, who succeeded him,

Marsha Wenk

Marsha Wenk grew up rooting for the underdog. The daughter of civil rights activists, she always kept fruit in her pocket to give to people on the street who asked for money. As the legal director for the ACLU-NJ in the 1990s, she continued to champion the underdog even after being diagnosed with pancreatic cancer in the spring of 1995. Wenk remained committed to her calling until her death at age 37 in March 1996.

"She was passionate and compassionate, intellectually sharp and open-minded," said Frances Bouchoux, a classmate of Wenk's at Rutgers School of Law-Newark and now the law school's associate dean for academic and student services. "She could always see the counter-argument, and that made her a great attorney."

The New Jersey native postponed her dream job — working for the ACLU-NJ — to get day-to-day trial experience. As a Warren County public defender, Wenk took on extra work to prove that a client's constitutional rights had been violated, even when the case could be resolved on far simpler grounds.

As the legal director of the ACLU-NJ, she left behind a storied legacy. Under Wenk's leadership, the ACLU-NJ challenged a plan to include prayers at a South Jersey school district's graduation ceremonies and established the right for one partner in a same-sex couple to adopt the other partner's children.

Wenk's commitment to justice lives on. Each semester, the Marsha Wenk Fellowship allows a Rutgers public interest law student to intern part-time at the ACLU-NJ, fulfilling the mission of an organization she loved and upholding principles she held so closely to her heart.

rolled most of his tax increases back. The state economy was buffeted by a recession in the early '90s, but made a strong comeback. New Jersey remained a prosperous state with a growing population. Underneath the gloss, though, there was worry about downsizing and layoffs.

By 1990 most ACLU-NJ litigation was in state courts, for the New Jersey constitution was seen as affording more individual liberty than comparable provisions in the federal Bill of Rights. Between 1990 and 2000 the ACLU-NJ worked on many cases challenging government attempts to restrict individual freedoms. It successfully defended Brien Desilets, for example, an eighth-grader in Gloucester County whose reviews of two R-rated movies were banned from the school newspaper. It got the state Department of Health to modify a rule that all children of married parents automatically get the father's name on their birth certificate. It limited police use of mobile data terminals to retrieve personal information on innocent motorists. And it tried — though without success — to kill a federal waiver allowing New Jersey to deny extra benefits to women who have more children after going on welfare (one of many instances in which the ACLU-NJ collaborated with strange bedfellows, in this case New Jersey Right to Life).

One of the stranger court fights of the era pitted the ACLU-NJ against Robert N. Wilentz, Chief Justice of the New Jersey Supreme Court from 1979 to 1996. Wilentz was known as a protector of the poor and the powerless, and a champion of individual rights. In the shopping mall case he delivered a passionate defense of free speech. But in May 1990 he assumed the unlikely role of censor by refusing to allow a movie company to shoot a scene from "The Bonfire of the Vanities" in a Newark courtroom. Wilentz said the scene — depicting blacks rioting after a judge ruled in favor of a white Wall Street trader — "could seriously undermine the confidence of black citizens in our court system." Essex County Executive Nicholas Amato sued Wilentz in federal District Court, saying the justice's actions cost Essex County $250,000 in fees. (The scene was eventually shot in New York.) The ACLU-NJ supported the lawsuit, claiming Wilentz had violated the First Amendment. Amato asked for damages, and requested an injunction preventing Wilentz from interfering with moviemakers in the future.

The judge ruled that Wilentz had indeed stepped on others' constitutional rights and violated First Amendment guarantees of free speech. But the Third Circuit Court of Appeals threw out the case in 1992, ruling that Essex County lacked the standing to sue. The ACLU-NJ stuck to its guns, pointing out that the county lost the case on a technicality. "We won in the court of public opinion," ACLU-NJ legal director Deborah Ellis told the New Jersey Law Journal. "It illustrates how conservative the federal courts are because there was a clear violation of the Constitution."

Another novel First Amendment case involved a homeless man named Richard Kreimer, who sought the assistance of the ACLU-NJ in a dispute with the board of the Joint Free Public Library of Morristown. Though strictly local, the case stirred debate all over the country.

Kreimer was a regular at the library, but frequently exhibited annoying behavior. He talked to himself, was hostile to staff, stared at other patrons or followed them around, and had an offensive body odor. The library board responded by enacting new rules, and ejected Kreimer for violating them. The ACLU-NJ negotiated with the library on his behalf, saying the rules discriminated against the homeless. The library amended the rules, but kicked Kreimer out again. Kreimer filed a lawsuit against the library pro se, but was eventually represented by Bruce Rosen, a young volunteer attorney for the ACLU-NJ.

Rosen did not really want to litigate the case. While the library's former director had tolerated Kreimer, the new director was not so forgiving. "Richard needed a little extra patience and could be difficult at times, but had a right to sit there," Rosen later recalled. "The new crew was not the least bit sympathetic. We tried talking to them numerous times, but they were done talking by the time we got there. They had drawn a line in the sand."

The lawsuit challenged the library's rules, crafted with Kreimer in mind. They required all patrons be engaged in reading, studying, or using library material, forbade staring and talking to oneself and barred library users "whose bodily hygiene is so offensive as to constitute a nuisance to other persons."

A sympathetic District Court judge ruled in his favor in 1991, saying library policy violated Kreimer's First Amendment right to "receive" ideas from the library's books and periodicals. The library's insurer settled with Kreimer for $80,000, but the library appealed the decision. The Third Circuit Court of Appeals reversed the following year, declaring the library had not violated Kreimer's rights and that the rules were both reasonable and valid. "A library is a place dedicated to quiet, to knowledge, and to beauty," the appeals court said. As a limited public forum, it "need not be used as a lounge or a shelter."

The ACLU-NJ did not pursue an appeal. Within the library community, as well as among homeless advocates, the Morristown Library case provoked endless debate. Libraries all over the country struggled to come up with constitutionally permissible rules of conduct.

Since its founding, the ACLU-NJ has fought consistently for the two prongs of religious freedom rooted in the First Amendment, protecting the individual's right to exercise his or her beliefs and preventing the government from endorsing any one religion. The goal is for the government to demonstrate neutrality toward religion, neither discriminating against nor endorsing religions or religious practice.

Much of the time, a phone call or letter quickly settles disputes concerning the separation of church and state, especially those of a symbolic nature. During the 1992-93 holiday season, for example, the ACLU-NJ wrote a dozen local and county governments after receiving complaints about crèches and menorahs on public lawns or steps. All dismantled their displays, or removed them to private property. The next year brought a case that was not so easily settled. The place: City Hall, Jersey City.

The legal battle began in 1994, when the ACLU-NJ filed a federal lawsuit challenging Jersey City's 30-year-old practice of displaying a menorah and nativity scene on the front lawn of City Hall during Hanukkah and Christmas. After a judge ruled that the city's display was unconstitutional, the city added a number of secular items — a plastic Santa Claus, Frosty the Snowman, a wooden sleigh, and an evergreen studded with Kwanzaa ribbons. A sign next to the display stated it was part of the city's year-long celebration of diversity. The ACLU-NJ challenged the new approach, and before long everyone was back in court.

ACLU v. Schundler ping-ponged between the District Court and the Third Circuit Court of Appeals for the next two years. A law firm, the Becket Fund for Religious Liberty in Washington, D.C., represented the city free of cost. Jersey City Mayor Bret Schundler began soliciting donations in 1998, fearful that the city could lose and be required to pay fees for the opposing side. Nonetheless he continued to insist that city government had the right to celebrate religion. "We celebrate cultures as they are and don't 'white-out' religious elements," Schundler said.

The battle ended in February 1999 when an appeals court panel ruled that the city's blend of religious and secular symbols satisfied U.S. Supreme Court rulings upholding similar displays in Rhode Island and Pennsylvania.

Throughout the 1990s the ACLU-NJ challenged traditional legal assumptions about family life. One such case cropped up in 1993. The alleged injustice may have seemed small, but big principles were involved. "A silly judge did an old-fashioned thing. We challenged it," said Lawrence S. Lustberg, the cooperating attorney who handled the case for the ACLU-NJ. "The Supreme Court took our challenge seriously, and made it into an important case. It wrote a superb opinion."

The story started on July 4, 1991, when Karen Deremer of Washington Borough in Warren County, gave birth to a baby boy. She and the father, Alan Gubernat decided not to marry. At first Gubernat doubted he was the father, and was not named on the infant's birth certificate. Later, he requested blood tests to determine paternity. After learning the child, Scott, was indeed his son, Gubernat began building a relationship with him and requested joint custody. He also asked the court

Lawrence S. Lustberg, ACLU-NJ cooperating attorney, speaks with client Karen Deremer, whose 1995 case put mothers on equal legal footing with fathers when it comes to the names of their children.
(Star-Ledger photographs ©The Star-Ledger, Newark, NJ)

to change Scott's last name, from his mother's name to his. A judge agreed to the change, but Karen Deremer appealed. A lower court and appeals court both ruled against her, but the New Jersey Supreme Court disagreed. "It is the love of the parent, not the name of the parent, that binds parent and child," the justices ruled in 1995. "The Court is firmly convinced that today's decision is not only consistent with the best interests of the affected children, but also reflects the significant societal changes in women's rights."

The case had an unexpected, horrific postscript. One week later, on Mother's Day, Gubernat shot and killed Scott, 3, and himself in his home. At the time Gubernat had custody of the little boy on weekends or for one night a week. He left no note, but friends assumed the shootings were related to the court decision. Lustberg, Deremer's attorney, attended the funeral and stayed in touch with her for several years afterward. To this day he thinks about the case. "It just reminds you that these cases are not just about the ACLU, or the lawyers, or the legal principles. These are about real human beings," he said later. "It also shows you something else. Any client who is willing to step forward and challenge always takes certain risks."

ACLU-NJ legal director Marsha Wenk, deeply troubled by the outcome of the case, said the ACLU had never questioned Gubernat's love for his child. "Certainly this was not something we would have expected," she said. "It is not a rational response to a court ruling that in no way threatened his continued relationship with the child. We are horrified by the tragedy."

A happier ending was in store for a gay couple from Maywood whose decision to start a family was thwarted by the policy of the N.J. Division of Youth and Family Services. At the time, gay family relationships were just beginning to be recognized. The child welfare agency approved Jon Holden and Michael Galluccio as foster parents, and placed a baby who was born HIV positive in their home. The infant, Adam, flourished under their love and care. But when the couple petitioned the state for consent to

Jon and Michael Galluccio successfully contested state regulations in 1997 that prohibited same-sex couples from adopting in a single joint proceeding. (Star-Ledger photographs © The Star-Ledger, Newark, NJ)

adopt Adam, they were told unmarried parents could not adopt together. If they wished to keep Adam, Michael would have to adopt him alone; Jon, the stay-at-home parent, would have to adopt him months later, in a separate procedure. The couple decided to press for joint adoption, and asked the ACLU-NJ to represent them.

In October 1997 a family court judge allowed the couple to jointly adopt the child, heeding the ACLU-NJ's argument that a two-step adoption policy was discriminatory. Adam Holden Galluccio was now two years old. The ruling was hailed in the gay community as a tremendous advance in gay adoption. Officials with the Division of Youth and Family Services subsequently revised their policy to permit unmarried couples — gay or straight — to jointly adopt children, just like married couples. "This all started out with Adam and two fathers trying to protect their son," Holden said at a news conference announcing the agreement. "What we have now is a recognition that there are many different kinds of families."

The couple went on to adopt a little girl and her older sister. In 2001 Jon and Michael Galluccio published a book about their lives called "An American Family."

James Dale sued the Boy Scouts of America in 1992 for kicking him out because he is gay.

As far back as 1983 the ACLU-NJ lobbied the state Legislature to outlaw discrimination against gays and lesbians. That finally happened in 1991, when legislators amended the New Jersey Law Against Discrimination by adding sexual orientation to protected characteristics such as race and religion in areas such as employment, housing and public accommodations. It was not long before the law was tested.

The case involved an assistant Scoutmaster from New Jersey named James Dale, who sued the Boy Scouts of America in 1992 for kicking him out because of his sexual orientation. Dale got involved in scouting at the age of eight, when he joined Cub Scout Pack 142 in Monmouth County. Three years later he became a Boy Scout, and while in high school he became an Eagle Scout, the organization's highest rank. Around the time Dale went off to college, he applied for adult membership in the Boy Scouts and became an assistant Scoutmaster. While at Rutgers, Dale became active with the Rutgers University Lesbian/Gay Alliance. A reporter interviewed Dale while covering one of the group's

Richard Rivera

When Richard Rivera was sworn into the West New York Police Department in 1990, he was determined that his career in law enforcement would have a positive impact.

Rivera achieved his goal, but not by sweeping criminals off the street. It came instead in 1994 through his courage in calling the FBI, letting the agency know about the unchecked corruption in the West New York Police Department.

The phone call resulted in the largest investigation of police corruption in New Jersey and led to the indictment of 34 people, including the police chief, on charges of accepting bribes to protect prostitution, illegal gambling, illicit liquor sales and extortion from towing companies. But instead of being praised for doing the right thing, Rivera was fired. He looked far and wide across the state for help in filing a lawsuit against the department's retaliation. Hardly anyone returned his calls except for the ACLU-NJ, which showed him how to access the information he needed for his lawsuit.

The town settled the lawsuit, but refused to admit any wrongdoing. Since then Rivera has advised the ACLU-NJ on cases concerning police affairs and co-authored the 2009 ACLU-NJ report, "The Crisis in Police Internal Affairs." As a former ACLU-NJ board member, he mapped out a 10-point plan on how to improve community policing and helped position the ACLU-NJ to become New Jersey's most powerful advocate for police accountability.

Today Rivera continues to make a difference in law enforcement, working as a consultant to assist victims of police corruption and to advise departments on better training and community outreach programs.

events, and quoted him in a newspaper article. He talked about gay teenagers needing gay role models. Within days Dale received a letter revoking his membership in the Boy Scouts. When he asked why, he was told Boy Scouts "specifically forbid membership to homosexuals."

Dale sued.

"Being proud about who I am is something the Boy Scouts taught me. They taught me to stand up for what I believe in," he said at the time. The ACLU-NJ, together with the Lesbian and Gay Rights Project of the ACLU, filed a friend-of-the-court brief arguing that the Boy Scouts was a "public accommodation" under the state anti-discrimination law that must treat all individuals equally. In 1999, the New Jersey Supreme Court agreed, and in a 7-0 decision rejected the Boy Scouts' claim that it was a private organization protected by the First Amendment. The court's opinion equated the Scouts' view of homosexuality with prejudice against women and blacks.

The Scouts appealed, and the U.S. Supreme Court sided with the Scouts in a 5-to-4 vote, saying the group had the constitutional right to exclude gay members because objecting to homosexuality was part of their "expressive message." The Scouts' famous pledge to be "morally straight," the court said, could be used to discriminate. (The Boy Scout oath says, "On my honor, I will do my best, To do my duty to God and my country and to obey the Scout Law; To help other people at all times; To keep myself physically strong, mentally awake and morally straight.")

"It appears that homosexuality has gained greater societal acceptance," the court wrote in the majority decision. "But this is scarcely an argument for denying First Amendment protection to those who refuse to accept these views. The First Amendment protects expression, be it of the popular variety or not."

During the next few months, the Boy Scouts of America lost support from corporations and foundations, and many Eagle Scouts returned their badges. A number of religious groups and volunteers also criticized the aggressive anti-gay stance. Dale's own reaction was muted. "I am very happy with the time I spent at the Boy Scouts. I am very sad about the direction the current leadership is taking them."

One perhaps unanticipated consequence of the ruling was that the Boy Scouts were subsequently denied preferred use of many public buildings, such as schools, because government entities are prohibited from providing special privileges, such as renting their space at lower rates, to organizations that discriminate.

The U.S. Supreme Court legalized abortion in 1973 in the momentous *Roe v. Wade* decision. Nearly 25 years later the New Jersey Legislature, riding a national wave of anti-abortion sentiment, restricted the right to abortion with two new laws. The first, adopted in 1997, outlawed what its sponsors called "partial birth" abortions. The second, passed in 1999, required teenagers to notify at least one parent before seeking an abortion. Lawyers with the ACLU-NJ teamed up with Planned Parenthood and blocked both statutes from taking effect.

The term "partial-birth abortion" was coined in the mid-1990s and quickly became part of the national vocabulary. It referred to a rarely-used abortion procedure known medically as "intact dilation and extraction," typically performed between the 19th and 26th week of pregnancy, often in situations where the mother's health is at risk.

New Jersey's partial-birth abortion bill was similar to legislation enacted in a number of other states, defining the procedure as "an abortion in which the person performing the abortion partially vaginally delivers a living human fetus before killing the fetus and completing the delivery." Congress also enacted a similar bill, but President Clinton vetoed it.

The Republican-controlled state legislature had originally passed the bill in June 1997, but Gov. Christine Todd Whitman, a pro-choice Republican, vetoed it. Her attorney general, Peter Verniero, said it could be unconstitutional. When the General Assembly and the state Senate voted to override her veto, she said her administration would not defend the law. Legislative leaders went out and hired their own lawyer.

Minutes after the Senate vote to override Whitman's veto, the ACLU-NJ filed a constitutional challenge in federal court arguing that the ban was so broadly defined that it could be applied to any abortion procedure after the first trimester. "The moment they voted, we ran over to the courthouse and filed our papers," said Lenora Lapidus, legal director of the ACLU at the time. "We had, of course, been very actively lobbying against it, and we had all our legal papers ready." A federal judge issued a temporary restraining order on the ban the next day. The judge, Anne E. Thompson, eventually struck down the law, declaring the measure unconstitutional because it failed to make exceptions for cases in which the mother's health was at risk. Lapidus had argued that the law constituted a virtual ban on abortions, as most abortion procedures could result in complications, forcing doctors to use the outlawed method. On appeal the Third Circuit Court of Appeals also ruled the law unconstitutional. In 2003, the U.S. Congress passed a partial-birth abortion law, and it was upheld by the U.S. Supreme Court in 2007.

Whitman signed New Jersey's Parental Notification for Abortion Act into law in 1999. It required an unmarried girl under 18 to notify a parent before having an abortion. But it also provided for a judicial waiver. A girl who was afraid of telling a parent could ask a judge to waive parental notification in a confidential hearing.

This time Lapidus filed the challenge in state court, contending the law would force some teenagers to have unwanted children or seek abortions elsewhere. There was last-minute drama when a Superior Court judge turned down the ACLU-NJ's request for an injunction. Health officials and abortion clinics rushed to comply with the law. On the evening before it was to take effect, a New Jersey Supreme Court judge halted its implementation pending a review of the law by the full court. The court ultimately struck down the law, saying it violated the equal protection guarantee of the state constitution by imposing a burden on girls wanting abortion that it did not impose on those who chose to have their babies.

In April 1999, something startling happened.

Governor Whitman and her attorney general conceded — for the first time — that some state troopers were targeting black and Hispanic drivers on the highway and searching them. They announced that a two-month study of motor vehicle stops by the state documented that at least 77 percent of the motorists asked to consent to a search of their car were minorities. "(It is) a problem that is more complex and subtle than we first realized," Whitman said.

Yet allegations about racial profiling had bubbled out of New Jersey for years. Black and Latino drivers had complained about troopers pulling them over for no reason. In 1996 a trial court judge in Gloucester County had even thrown out drug charges against 17 black defendants arrested along the southern end of the New Jersey Turnpike after ruling that state police selectively, and illegally, enforced the law. "The eradication of illegal drugs from our State is an obviously worthy goal, but not at the expense of individual rights," Superior Court Judge Robert Francis wrote in the 1996 ruling. The U.S. Justice Department took note of his decision — which the state appealed — and launched its own investigation.

Then came the turnpike shootings of the night of April 23, 1998, when two state troopers fired 11 shots into a van carrying four unarmed young men of color. The driver was taking the group to a basketball tryout in North Carolina when troopers pulled them over. When the occupants made "furtive movements," the troopers started firing. Three of the van's four occupants were wounded and hospitalized. The New Jersey State Police again vigorously denied charges of racial profiling. Finally, Col. Carl Williams, the state police superintendent, said in an interview published in The Star-Ledger that "mostly minorities" traffic in drugs. That was going too far. The governor fired Williams for being "racially insensitive." The ACLU-NJ, involved in ongoing litigation against the state police on behalf of 12 minority drivers, asked people who believed they had been stopped because of profiling to contact them.

Some doubted the sincerity of the governor and her chief law enforcement official, Peter Verniero. Whitman was pondering a run for U.S. Senate, and Verniero was facing confirmation hearings on his nomination to the New Jersey Supreme Court. In the end, it hardly mattered, for a federal judge was about to step into the picture. In December 1999 the U.S. Justice Department announced it would appoint a federal monitor to supervise an overhaul of the New Jersey State Police.

But the ACLU-NJ felt more needed to be done and continued to challenge the practice in the next decade.

CHAPTER SIX

Attack on American Soil

Fresh Threats to Civil Liberties

After the Sept. 11 attack, ACLU-NJ Executive Director Deborah Jacobs led the organization in a number of challenges to the government over violations of privacy and the right to due process. (New Jersey Law Journal)

eborah Jacobs had barely settled into her seat for the morning session of a conference on racial profiling in Atlantic City when someone strode up to the moderator and whispered into his ear. A second interruption came a few minutes later, followed by a startling announcement: "A plane has crashed into the World Trade Center in Manhattan. The conference is canceled."

Scores of law enforcement personnel, including New Jersey Attorney General John Farmer Jr. and State Police Superintendent Carson Dunbar, hurried from the room, stone-faced. Jacobs, the 33-year-old executive director of the American Civil Liberties

Union of New Jersey, and a colleague, King Downing, headed toward their car and threaded their way around the phalanx of police cars speeding north. On the way to Newark she turned on the radio, hoping for news that would make sense out of what was happening. With each update, her anxiety grew. *Terrorists hijacked two jets earlier this morning and flew them into the World Trade Center . . . A third hijacked plane has crashed into the Pentagon . . . U.S. airspace is shut down . . . The Twin Towers have collapsed and dissolved into a huge cloud of ash . . . A fourth hijacked plane has crashed in Pennsylvania.*

When Jacobs reached Newark, she dropped Downing off at his home. Then she went to her office, where stunned staffers huddled around a television. Most spent the afternoon making sure friends and family members were safe, as early reports on the death toll in New York rose past 6,000, more than twice the actual number. The calamity of 9/11 seemed certain to mark their personal lives forever. But it also took the work of the ACLU-NJ in a new direction.

On the day of the attacks President George W. Bush promised a fierce response, warning the government would make "no distinction between the terrorists . . . and those who harbor them." Nine days later, in a televised address to Congress and the nation, Bush used the term "war on terror," and said authorities would use "every tool of intelligence, every instrument of law enforcement" to disrupt the al-Qaeda terrorist network. The FBI began rounding up non-citizen Muslim, Middle Eastern and South Asian men as "persons of interest" and detaining them in secret, with little or no regard for due process.

On Sept. 26, 2001, the ACLU-NJ board of trustees adopted a resolution warning against victimizing innocent people because of their appearance or ancestry. "Targeting people based on their race does not become less of an act of baseless hatred just because it is done by police," the resolution read. "The ACLU backs the most energetic efforts to bring to justice the murderers who committed these acts. We are confident that this can be done in the name of a proud and free nation that will not compromise its most sacred principles to accommodate the acts of terrorists."

Within weeks, however, it appeared that the government was indeed sacrificing principles. Northern New Jersey became a hotbed of federal terrorism investigations. The U.S. Immigration and Naturalization Service continued to sweep up immigrants suspected of having ties to terrorism and hold them in secret. In an effort to reach the detained immigrants, ACLU-NJ attorneys used state right-to-know laws to request the names, ages and nationalities of detainees housed in the Passaic and Hudson County jails. When the counties refused to disclose the information, the ACLU-NJ sued in state court.

Challenging secret detentions was only one piece of the new agenda. On Oct. 26, 2001, President Bush signed the USA Patriot Act into law, radically expanding the federal government's surveillance and investigative powers. Concerned about the Patriot Act's impact on civil liberties, the ACLU-NJ embarked on a sustained public education campaign to inform the public about the new law. The affiliate also joined a campaign lobbying the governing bodies of New Jersey counties and municipalities to adopt resolutions rejecting provisions of the Patriot Act that violated civil liberties.

Throughout this period, Jacobs felt her own role changing. She had embarked on a career with the American Civil Liberties Union in 1992 and arrived in New Jersey from eastern Missouri in 1999. "I had always seen myself as sort of a 'bridge' advocate, carrying the torch during times of relative social and political calm. We worked as hard as any generation of advocates, but we didn't have a significant people's movement behind us," she reflected years later. "After 9/11, I realized I would have the opportunity to lead in a time of true crisis and unrest, which was an exciting prospect and a daunting challenge." As it turned out, the crisis triggered an era of remarkable growth for the ACLU-NJ. Under Jacobs' leadership, membership rose from 6,000 to 15,000; the number of staffers rose from 4 to 15; and the annual budget swelled to nearly $2 million.

The first hint of the secret detentions came shortly after 9/11, when the ACLU-NJ started getting calls about Muslim men who had gone missing from their communities. Their families surmised they had been picked up by the INS, which had contracts allowing it to house immigration violators in two federal detention facilities and three county jails in New Jersey. One of those jails, the Passaic County Jail in Paterson, was believed to hold the single largest group of detainees in the country. Before Sept. 11, 2001, the jail held an average of 50 immigration detainees; by December 2001, it housed 417, according to statistics later released by the U.S. Department of Justice.

The ACLU-NJ was concerned about the post-9/11 detainees for two reasons. By using immigration violations as a basis for detention, the Justice Department was trying an end run around constitutional requirements governing criminal investigations. U.S. Attorney General John Ashcroft had made no secret of his plan to put in place very strict and unorthodox enforcement of immigration laws. "The policy was, if you're out of status even one day, we will arrest you and hold you as long as we can," recalled former ACLU-NJ staff attorney J.C. Salyer, who began working on behalf of the detainees soon after 9/11. ("Out of status" is the government's term for failing to observe immigration regulations.)

There were also allegations of abuse. "They were basically being held incommunicado. There were a lot of problems with their making phone calls, or contacting legal representatives," Salyer said. "These were mostly people who had come to the U.S. because they loved it and wanted to make a life here. They had basically taken hard jobs, were not making a lot of money, and were being treated in this incredibly harsh way. There was this assumption they were terrorists until it was proved that they weren't."

One month after the Sept. 11 terrorist attack, ACLU-NJ attorney J.C. Salyer was given access to immigrants who were rounded up and detained in county jails. (Amanda Brown)

The ACLU-NJ worked with other advocacy organizations like the American Friends Service Committee to gain access to detainees. At first authorities refused to allow them inside the jails, even when families had given them the name of a specific inmate. "It was sort of a Kafkaesque, Catch-22 situation," Salyer said. "They came up with excuses, or said we didn't have the right form." In 2003, a report by the Justice Department's Office of the Inspector General acknowledged detainees had problems contacting attorneys in the days after Sept. 11.

In October 2001, however, the Passaic County Jail allowed Salyer and one other advocate inside. They found a group of dispirited men who had spent over a month in custody without quite understanding why. Salyer explained who he was, told them he was interested in finding out who they were, and asked if there was any way he could help. He could almost feel hope begin to flicker in the room. "It was the first time they were allowed to feel that they were victims in the situation. You could sense a real sense of relief that now, maybe, something would be done," he said. "Being able to tell them this was an amazing feeling."

On Nov. 28, 2001, with confusion still reigning over the number, identity and location of detainees, ACLU-NJ attorneys sent right-to-know requests to the Passaic and Hudson County jails seeking a list of all persons placed in custody since Sept. 11. The jails refused to reveal any information. The affiliate sued both counties on Jan. 22, 2002, citing a number of New Jersey laws, including an old statute unearthed by ACLU-NJ cooperating attorney Howard Moskowitz. The law, dating back to 1898, required that names of county inmates and their dates of incarceration be made public. A Superior Court judge ordered the jails to release the names. But the federal government stepped in and issued an "emergency" regulation overriding state law — and prohibited disclosure of any detainee information not approved by the federal government. ACLU-NJ attorneys challenged the government's authority to issue the regulation, but lost its appeal. The New Jersey Supreme Court refused to hear the case.

On March 6, 2002, the ACLU-NJ launched a separate battle in federal court to open the detainees' immigration hearings to

In 2002, protesters march outside the Passaic County Jail, which was believed to hold the largest group of detainees in the country after the 9/11 attacks. (DRUM – Desis Rising Up & Moving)

the press; the hearings had been closed on Sept. 21, 2001, under an emergency order issued by Michael Creppy, the chief federal immigration judge. The "Creppy Memo" prohibited members of the public, press or families of those facing deportation from observing hearings. Plaintiffs in the lawsuit, the North Jersey Media Group (publishers of The Record and The Herald News) and the New Jersey Law Journal, argued that the Creppy memo violated their constitutional rights to cover proceedings. While a federal District Court judge agreed, saying the case presented "a clear case of irreparable harm to a right protected by the First Amendment," an appeals court overruled him.

The decision to keep the hearings secret was at odds with a federal appeals court ruling in a similar case brought by the ACLU of Michigan on behalf of the Detroit Free Press. That panel of judges held that the Bush administration acted unlawfully by making deportation hearings secret. "Democracies die behind closed doors," it noted. Many observers hoped the U.S. Supreme Court would take up the matter and resolve the conflict, but it did not. To this day ACLU-NJ legal director Edward Barocas believes the courts at the time feared making a ruling that would undermine attempts to keep the country safe. "Our country and this region were shaken by the events of September 11, and the judges were understandably not immune to that. In those first cases, judges were fearful that any decision they made could negatively affect our country's security," he said in 2011. "The government stoked those fears" by arguing it needed to operate in secret.

In time, as the government released or deported the people it had taken off the street, the detainee issue subsided. But the ACLU-NJ continued its outreach within New Jersey's Muslim communities. In 2003, it hired attorney Parastou Hassouri as an immigrant rights specialist. By then the federal government's "Special Registration" program for Arab and Muslim men, begun in 2002 by the fledgling Department of Homeland Security, was fully under way. The program required thousands of mainly Arab and Muslim men to register with immigration authorities for fingerprinting and interviews. Hassouri worked to build relationships with New Jersey's immigrant communities and helped coordinate a "Know Your Rights" program.

Years later she vividly recalled the climate of fear affecting Muslims living in places like Paterson and Jersey City. But she also recalled encountering a deep sense of betrayal. Before 9/11, they had been proud to call the U.S. home. "They couldn't imagine that a country which was supposed to stand for justice could make rules that would categorically apply to people on the basis of their national origin only. It seemed very unfair and un-American," Hassouri said. "Many families who had been caught in the dragnet were forced to contemplate taking their U.S.-born children back to a country they had never known, because the father and breadwinner was going to be deported based on an immigration violation."

In challenging the Bush administration's response to domestic terrorism, the ACLU-NJ charted new territory. But it did not expend all its energy in that direction. It also advocated for long-standing causes such as gay rights, it advocated for improved police accountability and issued a series of research reports challenging state and local policies. In one report, the ACLU-NJ found that one in four New Jersey public schools illegally requested information designed to reveal the immigration status of children seeking to enroll. The New Jersey Department of Education responded by sending corrective letters to districts. Another report documented how effectively local police departments processed internal affairs complaints against police from civilians. The affiliate also launched a major initiative to strengthen citizen access to public records called the "Open Governance Project," an outgrowth of the post-9/11 fight against government secrecy. It successfully petitioned the U.S. Justice Department to investigate the Newark Police Department

Laila Maher

A shocking, violent experience at the hands of New Jersey state troopers during a traffic stop still makes Laila Maher emotional many years later. A trooper held a gun to her head, twisted her arm behind her back and threw her against the car. Another officer choked Maher's friend who had been in the car with her, Felix Morka, a Nigerian national who police repeatedly slammed head-first against the steering wheel.

Anger surged when Maher, an Egyptian-American, described what she had seen in the rearview mirror that night. The troopers behind her were laughing after they let them go, having given her friend a speeding ticket.

"Overnight, I became scared to death when I saw a police officer. My heart would race," said Maher, who had just graduated from law school in January 1996.

When State Police tried to prevent her from filing a complaint and later, after they found "no wrongdoing," Maher turned to the ACLU-NJ. Information the ACLU-NJ uncovered showed the abuse happened not at the hands of two rogue cops, but from a statewide policy training troopers to discriminate based on skin color. In January 2003, the state — which by then had acknowledged widespread racial profiling and agreed to federal monitoring — settled with Maher and other victims.

Two months later, Maher watched as Gov. James McGreevey made racial profiling a crime.

"That was the most healing moment," said Maher, who became director of Columbia University's Office of Equal Opportunity and Affirmative Action, as well as an ACLU-NJ member.

for civil rights violations against citizens. And it continued to represent dozens of individuals in common, everyday situations in which their civil liberties were threatened.

One such case involved a 14-year-old from Oceanport, Ryan Dwyer, who dared to criticize his school in a web page created on his home computer. School officials harshly disciplined him for his criticisms of the Maple Place School, where he was in eighth grade. "Down with Maple Place," Dwyer wrote across the top of the site. "This page is dedicated to showing students why their school isn't what it's cracked up to be." Dwyer's web page included links to various music groups, to web pages describing students' constitutional rights, and to a site dedicated to body piercing. In his own writings he called the school's principal a "dictator," complimented one teacher while mocking another, called disrupting class "fun," and encouraged classmates to express their "hatred" for Maple Place in a guestbook. The teenager also warned against using profanity: "NO PROFANITY (that's curse words and bad words) and no threats to any teacher or person EVER."

Maple School administrators discovered the site five days after it appeared. Oceanport's superintendent of schools called the boy's parents, and said Ryan was suspected of creating a page with "criminal content." He was suspended for a week, ordered off the school baseball team for a month, and denied permission to go on a class trip. The school also omitted his name from an awards announcement. The ACLU-NJ sued in federal court, accusing Oceanport of violating Ryan's right to free speech. The judge agreed, noting that classmates had left crude comments on the site but that the teen had no control over their comments. He also dismissed the school board's claim that the web site had disrupted school.

"My parents and I are happy that the court did the right thing and upheld my free-speech rights," the teenager said after the ruling. "But it's a shame that in our free country students like me can be punished just because administrators don't like what we have to say."

In other First Amendment cases the ACLU-NJ advocated for or sued on behalf of a man threatened with criminal charges because his neighbor heard him cursing; a union member cited for violating a municipal sign ordinance after displaying a 10-foot-high inflatable rat at a union rally; and a first aider removed from her volunteer fire department for expressing concern about staffing shortages at a public forum.

But few free speech cases had as great an impact as *The Committee for a Better Twin Rivers v. Twin Rivers Homeowners' Association*, a lawsuit affecting every homeowner living in a private community run by a homeowner association. In New Jersey, that meant more than a million people.

Twin Rivers is a community of 10,000 people spread over 719 acres in East Windsor, near Exit 8 of the New Jersey Turnpike. Homeowners who purchase property automatically become members of the Twin Rivers Homeowners' Association, a private corporation that governs the complex and provides services like snow removal and garbage pickup. In 2000, a group of homeowners brought a lawsuit in state court against their governing board for violating their constitutional rights. The lawsuit, designed to test the power of community associations, contested some of the Twin Rivers Homeowners' Association's rules, including those restricting lawn signs, limiting access to a community room, dictating the content of the association newsletter, and denying homeowners' voting rights.

The case, litigated by Frank Askin of Rutgers' Constitutional Litigation Clinic, wound its way through the courts for seven years before reaching the New Jersey Supreme Court in 2007. In a unanimous decision, the state's highest court ruled that Twin Rivers' rules did not violate New Jersey's constitutional guarantees of free expression. But, in an opinion that sets New Jersey apart from all other states, it added that such associations do not have carte blanche to prohibit residents' free speech rights. Rules must be "reasonable as to time, place and manner."

Askin declared a partial victory. "Residents of homeowners' associations seeking free speech rights within their communities lost the immediate battles, but may have won the war," he wrote in a commentary published the next day. "The Court said that residents of common-interest communities in New Jersey may 'successfully seek constitutional redress against a governing association that unreasonably infringes their free speech rights.'"

Just as the 1960s were a turning point in the civil rights movement and the 1970s a defining moment for women's rights, so was the decade from 2000 to 2010 a watershed for recognition of lesbian, gay, bisexual and transgender rights. During this period the ACLU-NJ successfully sued to have both names of same-sex partners appear on their child's birth certificate. It persuaded the state courts to grant a divorce to two women who had been legally married in Canada, rather than order a "dissolution of a civil union." The ACLU-NJ went to bat for the right of a lesbian high school couple to be nominated "Best Senior Couple," got rid of graduation dress codes specifying "dresses for girls, pants for boys," and participated in the lawsuit that established civil unions. It also got involved in a lawsuit over the use of the Ocean Grove Boardwalk Pavilion.

The Boardwalk Pavilion in Ocean Grove, a charming community on the Jersey Shore, is a popular local venue. It is a place to rest, meet friends, listen to music, pray or seek shelter from the sun and rain. For a modest fee, payable to the Ocean Grove Camp Meeting Association, the Methodist group that owns the property, the public can rent the structure for important events, such as weddings, baptisms and memorial services. When the state Legislature voted to recognize civil unions for same-sex couples in 2006, Harriet Bernstein and Luisa Paster decided to celebrate their civil union at the pavilion. It was an obvious choice: They lived in Ocean Grove and had many friends in the area, the pavilion occupied a beautiful spot by the ocean, and it had a roof to protect guests in case of bad weather.

Bernstein, a grandmother and retired school administrator, and Paster, a former academic librarian, had met seven years earlier at a retreat in the Poconos for Jewish gays and lesbians. "We came together like magnets," Paster once told a magazine reporter. In March 2007, a few months after the state gave its blessing to civil unions, they went to the office of the Camp Meeting Association to request a pavilion reservation. In the space used to describe the intended occasion, they wrote "civil union." "The young woman who took our application and deposit was lovely, and wished us very well," Paster recalled. "We left very happy. There was no indication anything was wrong. She said she just had to run it by the authorities."

The young woman telephoned later to say she couldn't process the application. When Bernstein asked why, she said the president of the association made the decision. Bernstein asked to speak with him. He didn't call, but did e-mail her with his reasons. "He said it went against the Book of Discipline of the Methodist Church to have a same-sex union in their churches," Bernstein said. The two women were hurt and angry, but didn't want to make, in her words, "a hullabaloo." In June 2007, the couple conferred with ACLU-NJ Legal Director Ed Barocas and Deputy Legal Director Jeanne

Luisa Paster and Harriet Bernstein celebrate their civil union on June 30, 2007, near a pavilion that refused same-sex unions. (Harriet Bernstein)

Terry Tan

Since 1987, Terry Tan has tended bar at the Golden Cicada tavern, a popular watering hole in Jersey City that he bought with his wife. For years, he turned down offers from developers to buy the land because they hoped to build a retirement home on the property.

However, in 1999, the Jersey City Redevelopment Agency adopted a plan that rezoned Tan's property for athletic or educational purposes. At the same time, St. Peter's Prep, a neighboring Catholic school, decided it needed Tan's land to complete a new football field. Tan was told to sell the property. He refused.

In 2005, the Jersey City Redevelopment Agency moved to seize his property, using eminent domain, to benefit St. Peter's Prep. The move violated the establishment clause of the Constitution, which forbids government entities from taking actions to aid a particular religious entity.

When the ACLU-NJ got involved, Jersey City and the redevelopment agency backed off.

The experience made Tan realize the importance of open government.

"The thing I learned from all of this is that you have to be vigilant and attend city hall meetings," Tan said. "Decisions are made by little groups of officials who decide who should be here and who shouldn't be here."

LoCicero, who agreed to represent them. Bernstein and Paster then filed a complaint with the New Jersey Division of Civil Rights alleging violation of the state's anti-discrimination law.

The civil rights division ruled in their favor, and dismissed the Camp Meeting Association's claim that a religious organization had the constitutional right to use its facilities in a way that was consistent with members' beliefs. When the association refused to settle, the case moved to the New Jersey Office of Administrative Law for a hearing. (The Methodist group also went to federal court to challenge New Jersey's jurisdiction in the case, but lost.) In Ocean Grove, meanwhile, a community known for its diversity and tolerance, hundreds rallied behind Bernstein and Paster and formed an organization, Ocean Grove United. One day, over 200 blue and yellow flags, symbolizing gay, lesbian, bisexual and transgender equality, popped up all over town in a show of support for the couple.

At the end of 2011, the case was still awaiting disposition.

In the meantime, Bernstein, 66, and Paster, 60, went ahead with their plans. They moved the venue for their ceremony to the fishing pier in Ocean Grove, a quarter of a mile from the pavilion, and sent invitations to 80 guests. On Sunday, June 30, 2007, 200 well-wishers showed up at the pier to celebrate their civil union.

The ACLU-NJ, which first became involved in the racial profiling issue in the late 1980s, continued to challenge the practice during this decade. During the 1990s — a period when state officials continued to deny the state police had a policy of racial profiling — it filed two lawsuits challenging the practice. Then, in 1999, New Jersey officials admitted that the practice of racial profiling existed, and the state entered into a consent decree with the U.S. Department of Justice, requiring management reforms within the state police. (The agreement was dissolved in 2009, after a new law established an office within the state attorney general's office to oversee the division of state police.) Under the legal agreement between the state and Justice Department's civil rights division, New Jersey promised to end racial profiling. The agreement required troopers on patrol to provide detailed documentation on all traffic stops. The decree established two federal monitors to oversee the reforms, but the ACLU-NJ decided it would follow the progress on its own. It commissioned a study of traffic stops on the southern end of the New Jersey Turnpike, and found that state troopers were continuing to stop black motorists at "greatly disproportionate" rates.

In 2003 New Jersey settled racial profiling lawsuits brought a number of years earlier by the ACLU-NJ, representing 12 persons of color stopped by troopers on the New Jersey Turnpike. The plaintiffs included Dr. Elmo Randolph, an African-American dentist from Orange who drove a luxury car and had been stopped and interrogated on the turnpike approximately 100 times — without ever getting a ticket. The court denied the ACLU-NJ's motion for class certification, but ultimately New Jersey agreed to pay $775,000 to the plaintiffs.

Starting in the 1990s, the ACLU-NJ went to court to challenge a new trend in legislation — laws restricting where sex offenders could live. A 1994 state law known as "Megan's Law" required them to register and get their parole officers' approval before moving into any apartment or house. Megan's Law — named after Megan Kanka, a 7-year-old Hamilton Township girl who had been raped and murdered in 1994 by a twice-convicted pedophile who lived across the street — also required authorities to notify the community when a sex offender moved into the neighborhood.

But the effort to toughen laws protecting children from known sex offenders did not stop with Megan's Law. Municipalities began passing local ordinances restricting where they could live. By 2005, numerous town councils had adopted laws creating "safe" zones around places where children were known to gather. A typical ordinance was adopted in Galloway Township outside Atlantic City; it barred convicted sex offenders from living within 2,500 feet of schools, playgrounds, parks and day care centers. The restriction effectively banned a Stockton State College student from living in his dorm, as well as anywhere else near the college. The student had been put on probation when he was 15 for having criminal sexual contact with a 13-year-old girl. Authorities classified him as a "Tier 1" offender, the lowest category of risk, and he had no other criminal history. Galloway's ordinance now meant he must leave the dorm, located within 2,500 feet of a day care center.

The ACLU-NJ represented him in a civil action challenging the exclusion, arguing that Megan's Law embodied a comprehensive set of mechanisms designed to protect society and provide for sex offenders' reintegration into society. The Galloway case was merged with a lawsuit against a similar ban in Cherry Hill and argued before the New Jersey Supreme Court. The state's highest court agreed with the ACLU-NJ's position and struck down both ordinances, saying they were pre-empted by Megan's Law. "How are you protecting the community by driving him 2,500 feet off campus?" one of the justices asked. "Do you think the fact that you've made him into a commuter makes the community any more safe?" The decision invalidated similar bans in scores of other towns.

Democracy depends on citizens knowing what government officials are doing, and New Jersey has two laws that are supposed to make this happen — the Open Public Meetings Act, passed in 1975, and the Open Public Records Act, revised in 2002. But because information is a source of power many elected officials and bureaucrats would prefer to keep it under their exclusive control.

In 2009, thanks to a grant from the Pratt Bequest Fund of Rutgers School of Law-Newark, the ACLU-NJ established an "Open Governance Project" to help New Jersey residents pry loose information to which they're entitled. The timing of the grant coincided with the economic downturn that crippled newsrooms nationwide, meaning there were fewer reporters to keep an eye on public officials. At the same time, the ACLU-NJ was receiving more complaints from citizens and bloggers who were shut out of public meetings or not allowed access to public records.

Most of the people who seek help from the project are ordinary folks prodded into action by a particular event. "Something has happened to make them citizen-activists. Before, they were really just Joe Public. They want information, and someone has denied them. They pick up the fight," said Bobby Conner, the project's first staff attorney. The ACLU-NJ has advocated on behalf of scores of citizens, including a Hackensack resident refused access to financial documents about a city contractor; a Union County man who

Carole Chiaffarano turned to the ACLU-NJ in 2010 after officials refused to release public planning records for a road-salt barn the township built in her neighborhood. (Amanda Brown)

was silenced by freeholders at a public meeting when he questioned them about nepotism; and a Newark man seeking salary information about employees of the Newark Housing Authority. (The housing authority stonewalled the man's requests for information six times, but relented after the ACLU-NJ threatened a lawsuit.)

Conner spent over a year advocating on behalf of Carole Chiaffarano, a Bethlehem Township resident who wished to delve into the history of a publicly financed road salt storage barn near her Hunterdon County home. She and other neighbors had opposed construction of the barn at township committee meetings, but it was built anyway. Chiaffarano later managed to obtain the original site plan from the town, but she suspected the township had submitted different plans to the various agencies from which it had to get permits. She therefore asked for equivalent records from the N.J. Department of Community Affairs. That's where she hit a brick wall. Chiaffarano contacted the ACLU-NJ, and it sued on her behalf. One month later, the state released the plans. The plans were in fact different from the ones Chiaffarano was provided by the town.

The ACLU-NJ has a long history of scrutinizing police practices, and not just with regard to racial profiling. In 1999 it issued a report describing a "Statewide Crisis in Policing." The report, drawn from newspaper accounts and civilian complaints, recommended New Jersey create an independent police review system. It also urged that all police agencies publicly release information relating to internal affairs investigations, civilian complaints, and money spent to settle misconduct and whistleblower lawsuits.

In 2004, the affiliate sued the police department in Manalapan Township, Monmouth County, for violating state discrimination laws. The lawsuit detailed an incident from 2003, when six boys — three of whom were black, and three white — were approached by police while socializing in a park. The African-American boys alleged police searched them without justification and berated them, but left their white friends alone. Their parents filed a complaint with Manalapan police; the officer taking the complaint described the boys as "negroes" on the form and dismissively shoved it into his back pocket after processing it. Although the police investigated, they took no further action. The township eventually paid $275,000 to settle the suit.

The ACLU-NJ also filed a pair of lawsuits in Newark, a city with a long history of police misconduct and a long record of ACLU-NJ litigation over the rights of citizens. The police misconduct issue heated up again in 2007 and 2008 when residents increasingly came to the affiliate with allegations of police misconduct. The first case involved Roberto Lima, publisher of the Brazilian Voice, a small newspaper in Newark, who sued police for violating his rights as a citizen and a journalist in a bizarre episode involving the discovery of a corpse. When a freelance photographer working for Lima went to the city's Ironbound neighborhood to photograph trash left behind after a Brazilian festival, the photographer discovered the body of a woman in a garbage-strewn alley and took pictures of it. According to the lawsuit filed by the ACLU-NJ Lima went to the scene and then notified police, who ordered him not to publish any photos, seized the photographer's camera, and demanded Lima turn over all originals and copies of the image. Lima offered them a complete copy set of the photos, but refused to turn over the originals. Police took him into custody and handcuffed him to a bench until he relinquished the photos. They also hassled his photographer, who did not speak English, about his immigration status — despite the fact that five years earlier, the Newark police had honored the photographer with a "Citizen of the Year" award for assisting them in solving crimes.

In the second case, two Newark boys, ages 13 and 15, and their 20-year-old Pop Warner football coach were placed in fear of their lives one rainy night while driving to get a burger in Newark after practice. As explained in a complaint filed by the ACLU-NJ, the coach was pulled over after he attempted to go around two stopped unmarked police cars in the street. Six officers allegedly leaped from the stopped cars with guns drawn and cursed at the group while searching them and the car. They found only football equipment. When the 13-year-old attempted to put money he was holding in his pocket, an officer threatened to "blow your f—g brains out." The coach protested their rights had been violated. "We do whatever we f—g want. We have no rules," another cop shouted. Police issued the coach tickets for not wearing a seat belt and for failing to change his driver's license from Missouri to New Jersey. Before leaving, they told the trio they were "lucky" to have gotten off so easily.

ACLU-NJ staff attempted to work with the City of Newark's Law Department to resolve issues and promote reforms, but the city was unwilling or incapable of addressing charges of unprofessional practices and rogue officers. To document the scope of the problem, the ACLU-NJ hired an attorney, Flavio Komuves, to comb through hundreds of civil and criminal court records, press clippings, city council minutes and statistics from Newark Police Internal Affairs Division for evidence of police misconduct between Jan. 1, 2008, and July 1, 2010. The results were shocking: 418 complaints of serious misconduct within the two-and-a-half year period. Just as striking was the fact that very few officers were punished for their actions.

On Sept. 9, 2010, the ACLU-NJ petitioned the civil rights division of the U.S. Department of Justice to investigate and appoint a monitor to oversee the Newark Police Department. Misconduct by police "has left citizens dead, permanently injured, and otherwise damaged," the 96-page document said. "And it has left (citizens) unsure whether an encounter with (the police) will lead to them being protected and served or beaten and arrested."

During the period under study, 64 lawsuits were filed against Newark police; about 60 percent involved claims of unconstitutional searches and seizures, excessive force, false arrest, or other misconduct. The city paid out $2.1 million to settle claims by civilians, and $2.8 million on claims of mistreatment from its own employees. The police department's internal affairs division, meanwhile, substantiated only one of 261 serious complaints it received.

Behind the numbers were dozens of allegations about hostile encounters. An unarmed driver who collided with a Newark police car and got into a fight with its occupants was shot and killed; the city paid $1 million to settle a claim by his estate. During a raid, a complaint alleged, police set fire to a sofa bed where a mother and her children were asleep, burning all three; the city settled for $250,000. Police stopped a motorist on an outstanding warrant, but did not tell him why. When the motorist asked, an officer struck him in the face; the city paid $60,000 to settle his claim. In another case, police threatened to throw a juvenile off a bridge for refusing to admit involvement in a crime. Then, instead of taking him home as ordered, they took him to a secluded location, beat him up and urinated on him, according to public records.

On May 9, 2011, the Justice Department announced it would investigate the claims of brutality, intimidation and false arrests by Newark police. Under a 1994 law, adopted after Los Angeles police were caught on tape beating Rodney King, who was stopped for speeding, the federal agency can order reforms of police agencies found to exhibit a "pattern or practice" of unconstitutional or illegal conduct. It has overseen investigations in many states, including New York, Ohio, Louisiana and California.

Jacobs, the ACLU-NJ executive director, said she hoped the intervention would give the department a fresh start. "The recurrent problems in the Newark Police did not arise from one individual, or even a group of individuals, but from an inherited institutional culture of misconduct," she said. "We hope this investigation marks the beginning of a new era."

Our society has changed radically since 1960, when the ACLU established an affiliate in New Jersey. Politically, culturally, technologically, the America of today is not the America of 1960.

Even so, the same conflicts over personal liberties that existed when the ACLU-NJ was founded exist today. They just play out in a dramatically different landscape. In the 1960s, governments used a myriad of tactics to quash Vietnam War protests and other types of free speech in the streets. Today, demonstrators who voice discontent in the Occupy Wall Street movement in New Jersey and across the country face similar obstacles as they try to assemble in public spaces. In the 1960s, we fought for equal treatment under the law for African Americans. Today, our statutes call for equality, but discrimination and disadvantage continue to afflict African-American and immigrant communities in the areas of criminal justice, voting rights, education and employment. And 50 years ago, the government used national security to justify spying on activists and citizens. Today, we've seen our rights to privacy — on the telephone, at the airport, at home and even in our libraries — slowly stripped away in the name of homeland security.

The 20th century's revolutions in technology have radically altered the battleground of the fight for our rights to free speech and privacy. As Internet and mobile phone technology progresses, so too will the government's ability to monitor private actions. Social media has revolutionized the way we interact with one another and provided a new forum for us to speak our minds and share our thoughts. At the same time, it has proven fertile ground for First Amendment disputes, testing the dividing line between personal speech and official opinion for teachers, police officers and other public employees. The ACLU has been at the forefront of cyber-liberties and will continue to lead the way as technology and social media evolve.

The ACLU-NJ has fought for decades to secure fair and humane practices in Newark and across the state. ACLU founder Roger Baldwin said, "No fight for liberty ever stays won," and his adage has proven as true for police accountability as it has for free speech. New technologies have an impact on policing, as well, and provide the ACLU with ample opportunity to shape policies on the use of technological tools with respect to civil liberties. In the short term, we hope to see the Department of Justice finally take hold of the Newark Police and give the city and its residents a chance to develop positive police-community relations. In the long term, we will continue to represent victims of police abuse and fight for statewide policies and practices that promote the safety of citizens.

The final chapter of legal equality for gays and lesbians in America is still being written, but momentum and progress of thought gives us hope. The opposition to marriage equality for gays and lesbians shrinks with each passing day as more Americans recognize that the current law relegates same-sex couples to second-class status. As of 2011, six states recognize marriages between same-sex couples. New Jersey is not one of them. We will change that.

The outlook for civil liberties has never followed a predictable trajectory. Every generation's demagogues present new claims to justify why this time is different through tired attempts to convince citizens to willingly part with their rights. The bogeyman changes, but the tactics more often than not remain the same. And with each new generation, the ACLU mounts new campaigns against the kind of fear-mongering and prejudice that always reveals itself more clearly in hindsight.

We have evolved beyond a society where vigilante groups preached white supremacy in Newark and teachers could be fired for refusing to recite oaths of loyalty to the U.S. government, in large part because the ACLU's vigilance in every state of the union reinforced our nationwide ideals of liberty for all.

America's history has been marked by surges of equality followed by resistance to progress. Ultimately, as Martin Luther King Jr. declared, "the arc of history is long, but it bends toward justice." Without the ACLU's unyielding defense of civil liberties, that arc would be much longer.

Deborah Jacobs
ACLU-NJ Executive Director
MARCH 2012

Index

Page numbers with italicized *ph* indicate photographs on the page.

A

abortion
 life armbands against, 3
 parental notification of, 95,
  96–97
 partial birth, 95–96
 prohibiting Medicaid-financed, 67
 rights, 50–51
ACLU v. Schundler, 88
acts of civil disobedience, 63–66
Adams v. Hughes, 31–32
Addonizio, Hugh J., 26, 30, 31
adoptions, by same-sex couples,
 90, 110
African-Americans. *See* blacks
AIDS, discrimination based on, 76
Amato, Nicholas, 86
American Civil Liberties Union
 (ACLU)
 first woman to assume leadership
  role, 29
 founding of, 11
American Civil Liberties Union of
 Michigan, 105
American Civil Liberties Union of
 New Jersey (ACLU-NJ)
 about, 1–4
 challenging response to domestic
  terrorism, 106, 108–110

civil rights dominating agenda
 of, 21–22
complaints shift to direct
 representation of clients, 32–33
expanding chapters of, 21
first president of, 16
goals of, 19–20
relationship with black
 community, 37
American Friends Service
 Committee, 103
American Jewish Committee, 8
Americans with Disabilities Act, 76
anti-Communist
 faction, 19
 paranoia, 40. *See also* McCarthy era
Anti-Nazi Act, 12
anti-war
 newspaper, 36
 prisoners, 36
 protesters, 22, 35, 81–83
 sentiment, 32
Arabs, 105–106
Army, U.S.
 desegregation of, 7
 investigation of installation by
  McCarthy, 18–19
 surveillance program of activists, 40

Ashcroft, John, 102
Askin, Frank, 34, 39–40, 47, 47*ph*,
   55, 61–62, 82, 109–110
Atlantic City, 37, 99, 115
Attica (NY), 53

B

Baby and Child Care (Spock), 33
Baer, Byron, 57–58
Baldwin, Roger N., 11, 13, 14, 15, 122
Baldwin Civil Liberties Award,
   Roger N., 9, 16
Balsley, Beth, 69–70, 69*ph*, 72
Barbaro, Fred, 21, 30
Barocas, Edward, 105, 111
battered woman syndrome, 68
Becket Fund for Religious Liberty
   (Washington, D.C.), 88
Bender, Bill, 34, 34*ph*
Bender, Rita, 34, 34*ph*, 37–38
Berger, Michael, 58–59
Bernstein, Harriet, 110, 111,
   111*ph*, 113
Bertin, Micah, 33*ph*
Bethlehem Township (NJ), 117
Bible
   compulsory public school
      readings of, 1, 21
   compulsory readings of, 64
Bill of Rights, New Jersey provision
   of, 8
birth certificate
   child's, 110
   infant's, 89
bisexual rights, 110, 113
blacklisted Hollywood actors, 18
blacks
   equality for, 121
   harassment of, 44, 49

integration of Levittown, 7, 8, 10
lynchings of, 6
1967 Newark rebellion and,
   23–26, 23*ph*, 28, 30–32
polling districts discriminating
   against, 21
racial profiling of, 97, 114, 118
relationship with ACLU-NJ, 26
segregation in Levittown, 5–8
Boardwalk Pavilion in Ocean
   Grove, 110
Boring, Phyllis Zatlin, 43
Bouchoux, Frances, 84
Boudin, Kathy, 27
Boy Scouts of America, 92, 94
Brazilian Voice (newspaper), 118
Bridgeton (NJ), 59
Brooklyn College, 20
Brown, Ozell, 31
Buckman, Bill, 44, 44*ph*
Burlington County and
   Willingboro chapters, 10
Bush, George H.W, 81
Bush, George W., 100, 101, 105, 106
Byrne, Brendan, 32

C

Cahill, William, 53–54
Camden, 2, 5, 37
Camden County, 76
Camden County Legal Services,
   Inc., 57, 58
Carlstadt-East Rutherford Regional
   School District, 78
   (El Comité de Apoyo a los
   Trabajadores Agricolas), 59
censorship, 2, 22
Center for Disease Control and
   Prevention, 76

Cherry Hill (NJ), 115
Chiaffarano, Carole, 116–117, 116*ph*
children
    busing parochial school, 17
    clinic for disabled, 55
    protecting from sex offenders,
        114–115
Christiano, Karen, 52
civil disobedience, acts of, 63–66
civil disturbances, 22, 39
The Civil Liberties Reporter
    (newsletter)
    on content of speech, 35
    on solving problems in ghetto, 38
civil liberties violations, 19, 58, 101
civil rights
    dominating ACLU-NJ agenda,
        21–22
    expanded, 17
civil unions, 110–111, 113. *See also*
    same-sex couples
civilian police review board, 22, 30
Clark, William, 14
Clinton, Bill, 83, 95
clubs
    eating, 69, 73
    secret Communist, 19
    selective private, 68
Coalition for Peace Action, 81
Collum, Joe, 80
Comite Organizador de Trabajadores
    Agricolas (COTA), 59
Committee Against Discrimination
    in Housing, 8
*The Committee for a Better Twin
    Rivers v. Twin Rivers Homeowners'
    Association*, 109
Communists
    FBI files on, 40
    fear of, 1

paranoia of, 17–18
surveillance of, 15
Community Legal Action
    Workshop (CLAW), 34, 37–38, 67
Congress of Racial Equality,
    Newark chapter of, 28, 30
Conner, Bobby, 116–117
conscientious-objector status, 35, 36
Constitutional Litigation Clinic, 47,
    49, 55
Cooperman, Saul, 65, 66
Corrado, Frank, 74
Cottage Club, 73, 75
Council on Human Relations, 8
Cox, Nancy, 13
Creppy, Michael, 105
cruel and unusual punishment,
    standard for, 54
curfews, 48
Curvin, Robert, 30, 31

D

Dale, James, 92, 92*ph*, 94–95
Darnell, Emerson, 6, 8–11, 9*ph*
Debevoise, Dickinson R., 65–66
Delaware (DE), random police
    stops, 61–62
demonstrators, 39, 121
Department of Homeland
    Security, 105
Deremer, Karen, 89–90, 89*ph*, 90
Deremer, Scott, 89–90
Desilets, Brien, 85
detainees, 101–104
Detroit Free Press, 105
di Suvero, Henry, 23–25, 23*ph*,
    27–29
Dintino, Justin, 80
discrimination. *See also* gender

equality cases
  based on HIV/AIDS, 76
  housing, 5–8, 11
  in occupied German restaurant, 7
  racial, 2
  against sexual orientation, 92,
    94–95
D'Joseph, Rita, 24, 27
Dominguez, Angel, 59
Douglas, Justice William O., 45
Downing, King, 100
draft
  cards, 35–36
  counseling, 2
  information centers, 36
Driscoll, Alfred E., 17
drug testing, mandatory, 78–79
drugs, 67, 97, 98. See also marijuana
Dunbar, Carson, 99
Dwyer, Ryan, 108

E

East Orange (NJ), 2
East Windsor (NJ), 109
Eastern Lawn Tennis Association, 52
eating clubs, 73, 75
Eatontown (NJ), 18
Edison Township Board of
  Education, 33
Edison Township (NJ), 63
Education and Defense Fund for
  Racial Equality, 37
Eighth Amendment violation, 54
The Electric Kool-Aid Acid Test
  (Wolfe), 47
Elizabeth (NJ), 33
Ellis, Deborah, 3, 86
Ellsberg, Daniel, 27

Englewood Board of Education
  (NJ), 18
Englewood Cliffs, 51
Equal Opportunity and Affirmative
  Action, 107
Essex County, 68, 86
Essex County Coordinating
  Committee, 30
Everson, Arch R., 17
Everson v. Board of Education, 17
Ewing Township (NJ), 17

F

Falwell, Jerry, 67
Farmer, John, Jr., 99
farmworkers, 2
Farmworkers Rights Project, 58–59,
  59, 59ph
Farmworkers Support Committee
  (Bridgeton), 59
FBI
  files on Communists, 40
  growth of, 15
  investigating communist clubs, 19
  investigating West New York
    Police Department, 93
  investigation of Paton, 60
  response to 9/11 attacks, 100
FHA (Federal Housing
  Administration), 7, 8
Fifth Amendment, 19, 43
film censorship, 2
First Amendment. See also free
  speech cases
  draft reclassifications and, 36
  fights against Hague, 1, 14
  libraries and, 87
  moment of silence and, 65
  obscene material and, 21

protection, 94
secret hearings and, 105
Florio, Jim, 80, 83
Fogel, Jeffrey, 36, 47–48, 65, 66–67
Fort Dix, 6–7, 36
Fort Monmouth, 18–19
Fourth Amendment, unreasonable
    search and seizure, 43, 55, 61,
    77–78
Francis, Robert, 97
Frank, Sally, 2, 69, 72–73, 73*ph*,
    75–76
Freamon, Bernard, 38–39
free speech
    defense of, 3
    restricting, 14, 15
    violations of, 39–40
free speech cases, 60–61, 108–110,
    109, 122
free speech rights, 12, 82, 110
freedom, religious, 71, 87–88
Freehold Board of Education (NJ),
    20–21
Freymire, Elwood, 46
Freymire, Kim, 46
Freymire, Marilynn, 46
Friends of New Germany, 12

G

Galloway Township (NJ), 115
Galluccio, Michael, 90, 91*ph*
Galluccio, Adam Holden, 90–91,
    91*ph*
Gans, Herbert J., 10
Garth, Leonard I., 52
Gay Rights Project, 94
gays
    adoptions by, 90–91, 110
    in Boy Scouts of America, 92,
        94–95
    condemnation of, 67
    discrimination based on HIV/
        AIDS, 76
    entrapment of, 9
    legal equality for, 122
    rights of, 2, 106, 110, 113
    at University of Wyoming, 83
gender discrimination cases, 41–43,
    45–46, 50, 69
gender equality cases, 51–52
German American Bund, 12
Gibson, Kenneth, 25, 25*ph*
Ginsburg, Ruth Bader, 42–43, 42*ph*,
    45–46, 50, 52
Glassboro Service Association (NJ),
    57, 58–59
Gleason, John, 31
Gloucester County (NJ), 85, 97
government endorsing religion,
    65, 88
Gross, Beth. *See* Balsley, Beth
Gubernat, Alan, 89–90

H

Hague, Frank, 1, 13–14, 13*ph*, 14
*Hague v. Committee for Industrial
    Organization*, 13
Hamilton Township (NJ), 114
Hassouri, Parastou, 105, 106
Hawaii, internment of Japanese
    Americans, 15
Hayden, Tom, 26
Hays, Arthur Garfield, 12, 14
hearings secret, making
    deportation, 105
Hennessey, James, 79

Henry P. Becton Regional High
School, 78
The Herald News, 105
Hershey, Lewis B., 35, 36
high school sports, gender equality
in, 48, 51–52
Hinds, Lennox, 53, 56
hippies, profiling, 47–49, 79–80
Hiroshima bombing, 16
Hispanics, racial profiling of, 9, 97
HIV/AIDS, discrimination based
on, 76
Hogan, Daniel, 54, 56
Holden, Jon, 90, 91*ph*
holiday season displays, 88
The Home News of New Brunswick, on
"mother's insurance" benefits, 42
Homeland Security, Department
of, 105
homeless in libraries, 86–87
Hoofprints (school newspaper), 74
House Committee on Un-
American Activities, 18, 19
housing discrimination, 1, 5–8, 11
Hudson County Jail, 101, 104
Hudson County (NJ), 13, 39
Hughes, Mildred Barry, 22
Hughes, Richard J., 21, 22, 25,
31–32
Hunterdon County (NJ), 117
Hussein, Saddam, 81

I

immigrants, detainee, 101, 102
Immigration and Naturalization
Service, U.S., 102
Imperiale, Anthony, 24, 25, 25*ph*,
26–27
integration, of Levittown, 8

Internal Affairs, 79
Internet technology, 121
Iraq, 81, 82
Italian-American North Ward
(Newark), 26
Ivy Club, 73, 75

J

Jacobs, Deborah, 99–100, 99*ph*, 101,
120, 121–123
James, Willie R., 6–8, 10
Japanese Americans, internment
of, 15
Jaycees and Lions International, 68
Jersey City, 12, 14, 76, 88
Jersey City Police Department, 39
Jersey City Redevelopment
Agency, 112
John P. Stevens High School
(Edison Township), 63
Johnson, Jerome, 6
Joint Free Public Library of
Morristown, 86–87

K

Kanka, Megan, 114
Katchen, Ira J., 19
Kean, Thomas H., 64–65
Kelly, Gladys, 68
Kelly, Oliver, 26
Kennedy, Robert F., 32
Kent State University (OH), 48
Kidd, Marian, 26
Kidd v. Addonizio, 26, 30–31
King, Martin Luther, Jr., 32, 123
King, Rodney, 120
Kinoy, Arthur, 46
Kiwanis Club of Ridgewood, 68

Knights of Columbus, 8
Know your Rights program, 106
Komuves, Flavio, 119
Kreimer, Richard, 86–87
Ku Klux Klan, 3, 9, 39
Kugler, George, 50–51
Kuhn, Estelle, 21
Kuwait, 81

L

Laba, Estelle, 15, 15*ph*, 19
Lapidus, Lenora, 96
Latimer, Steve, 54
Latinos, racial profiling of, 97
Lawrence Township (NJ), 82
leafleting, prohibiting, 82
left-wing groups, surveillance of, 15
lesbian rights, 110–111, 113, 122.
  See also gays
Lett, Harold, 10
Levine, Howard, 20
Levitt, William "Bill," 5–8, 7, 10
Levitt & Sons Inc, 6
*Levitt & Sons Inc v. Division Against
  Discrimination*, 8
Levittown (NJ), 5–8, 5*ph*, 7, 8, 10, 11
Levittown (NY), 5, 7
Levittown (PA), 5, 7
Lifset, Jane Z., 43, 45
Lima, Robert, 118
Lima, Roberto, 118
Linden (NJ), 33
Livingston, Robert M., 51
Livingston Mall, 82–83
LoCicero, Jeanne, 111, 113
Lofton, Oliver, 34
Long, Lester, 30
Los Angeles police, 120
Lowenstein, Robert, 19

loyalty oaths, 1, 17–18, 123
Lustberg, Lawrence S., 89–90, 89*ph*
lynchings, 6

M

Maher, Laila, 107, 107*ph*
Mainland Regional High School, 74
Malin, Patrick Murphy, 8
Manalapan police, 118
Manalapan Township (NJ), 117
mandatory drug testing, 78–79
Maple Place School, 108
marijuana, 32, 49, 61, 77, 79. *See
  also* drugs
Matthews, Robert A., 39
May, Jeff, 2, 63–66, 63*ph*, 70
May v. Cooperman, 66
Maywood (NJ), 90
McCarthy, Joseph, 17–19, 20, 28, 40
McCool, Maggie, 71, 71*ph*
McGreevey, James, 107
Megan's Law, 114–115
Mercer-Hunterdon ACLU
  chapters, 21
Meyers, Bill, 7
Meyers, Daisy, 7
Michigan, ACLU of, 105
migrant workers, 57
Military Park Hotel (Newark), 23, 27
Miller, Henry, 2
Millville (NJ), 3
misconduct by police, 118–120
moment-of-silence laws, 63–66
Monmouth (NJ), 21
Monmouth County, 22, 92, 117
Moore, Robert "Bob," 81–83, 81*ph*
Morka, Felix, 107
Morris (NJ), 21

Morris L. Ernst of New York
(attorneys), 14
Morristown (NJ), 86
Moskowitz, Howard, 104
Mosston, Leora, 56
"mother's insurance" benefits, 42
Murphy, Vincent, 17
Muslims, 100, 102, 105–106

N

N. J. Department of Community
Affairs, 117
N. J. Division of Youth and Family
Services, 90–91
NAACP, 8, 10, 30, 79
Nagler, Stephen, 28, 37, 57, 58
National Emergency Civil Liberties
Committee in New York (NY), 28
National Guard, during 1967
Newark rebellion, 24ph, 25–26
National Guardswoman,
discharging, 52
National Prison Project
(Washington, D.C.), 53
National Selective Service, 35
Nazi-friendly groups, 12
Neisser, Eric, 55, 78–79, 79
neo-Nazis, 3
New Brunswick (NJ), 37
New Jersey and New York
Communist, 15
New Jersey Department of
Education, 106
New Jersey Division of Civil
Rights, 73, 113
New Jersey Farm Bureau, 57
New Jersey Interscholastic Athletic
Association, 51
New Jersey Law Against

Discrimination, 68, 76, 92
New Jersey (NJ)
bans discrimination, 7
civil rights unrest in, 3
Law Against Discrimination, 8
McCarthyism in, 19
provision of Bill of Rights, 8
New Jersey Office of Administrative
Law, 113
New Jersey State Police. See also
Newark Police Department
harassment of long-haired men,
47–49, 79–80
during 1967 Newark rebellion, 26
profiling drivers, 79–80, 97–98,
107, 113–114
New York, National Emergency
Civil Liberties Committee in
New York, 28
New York City (NYC), Socialist
Labor Party in, 60
New York University and Harvard
Law, 20
Newark
1967 rebellion in, 2, 22, 22–26,
22ph, 28, 30–32
and Plainfield riots, 39
power structure in, 37
teachers accused of being
Communists, 19
Newark City Hospital, 30
Newark College of Engineering, 18
Newark Housing Authority, 18, 117
Newark Law Commune, 47
Newark Legal Services program, 25,
28, 38
Newark News
on Nancy Cox, 13
on Newark rebellion in 1967, 25
Newark Police Department. See also

racial profiling
  during 1967 rebellion, 25–26, 27
  changing relationship with, 122
  investigation of, 106, 108
  legal challenge to operation of, 31
  reaction to riots, 37
  "Red Squad" in, 13
  relationship with black
    community prior to 1967, 30
  urine testing from, 78
Newark rebellion (1967), 23–26,
  23*ph*
Newark teachers, 19
Newark's Mosque Theater, 15
9/11 attacks
  detentions after, 101–106
  on World Trade Center, 99–100
Nixon, Richard, 48
North Hunterdon High School,
  69, 70
North Jersey Media Group, 105
North Ward Citizens Committee, 23

O

obscene literature, 21, 22
Occupational Safety and Health
  Administration, U.S., 58
Occupy Wall Street, 121
Ocean Grove Boardwalk Pavilion,
  110–111
Ocean Grove United, 113
Oceanport (NJ), 108
O'Connor, Sandra Day, 67
Ohio National Guard, 48
Open Governance Project, 106, 116
Open Public Meetings Act, 115–116
Open Public Records Act, 115–116
Oxfeld, Emil, 11, 15–17, 15*ph*, 16*ph*,
  19–22, 35

P

Parental Notification of Abortion
  Act, 96–97
Parsippany-Troy Hills (NJ), 52
Passaic (NJ), 11
Passaic County Jail (Paterson), 101–
  106, 102, 104*ph*
Passaic County Sheriff's Office, 78
Paster, Luisa, 110, 111, 111*ph*, 113
Paterson (NJ), 11, 21, 102
Paton, Lori, 59–61
People's Electric Law School, 47
Philadelphia
  civil rights workers murdered
    near, 37
  police, 49
  Quakers as conscientious-
    objectors, 36
Piscataway Township (NJ), 77
Plainfield (NJ), 2, 31, 39, 78
Planned Parenthood, 95
police. *See also* New Jersey
  State Police; Newark Police
  Department
  brutality, 2, 28, 30, 31, 34
  lawlessness, 25–26
  review system, independent, 117
  surveillance lawsuit, first, 39
Pop Warner football league, 118–119
pornography, 21, 22
Pratt Bequest Fund of Rutgers
  School of Law, 116
prayers, in public schools, 21, 64, 84
Princeton (NJ), 50
Princeton University, 2, 69, 73, 75
Prisoner Rights Organized Defense
  (PROD), 53, 56, 67
profiling
  long-haired men, 47–49, 79–80

racial, 9, 44, 79–80, 97, 100–101, 107, 113–114, 118
pro-Nazi groups, 12, 13
public schools
  compulsory readings of Bible, 1, 21, 64
  prayer in, 21, 64, 84
  singing hymms in, 20
Puerto Ricans
  1974 riots by, 38
  picking crops, 57
  polling districts discriminating against, 21
  punishment, corporal, in prisons, 53–54

Q

al-Qaeda terrorist network, 100
Quakerbridge Mall (Lawrence Township), 82, 83
Quakers (Philadelphia), as conscientious-objectors, 36
Quran, burning of, 3

R

racial equality, 22, 28, 30
racial profiling, 9, 44, 79, 97, 100–101, 107, 113–114, 118
Rahway State Prison (NJ), 53–54
Randolph, Elmo, 114
Reagan, Nancy, 67
Reagan, Ronald, 67
The Record (newspaper), 105
"Red Squad," in Newark Police Department, 13
Rehnquist, William, 40, 61
religious freedom, 71, 87–88
Return of Law and Decency, 24

rights to privacy, 121
riots
  1974 Puerto Rican, 38
  1967 Newark rebellion, 23–26, 23*ph*, 28, 30–32
  prison, 53
  in Watts, 37
Ripston, Ramona, 23, 27, 28, 29, 29*ph*
Rivera, Richard, 93, 93*ph*
Robeson, Paul, 16
Roe v. Wade, 50, 51, 67, 95
Rosen, Bruce, 87
Rosenberg, Julius, 18
Rutgers Constitutional Litigation Clinic, 55, 109
Rutgers School of Law, Pratt Bequest Fund of, 116
Rutgers School of Law-Newark, 20, 45-48, 75
Rutgers University, 18
Rutgers University Lesbian/Gay Alliance, 92

S

St. Peter's Prep (Jersey City), 112
Salyer, J. C., 102–103, 103*ph*
same-sex couples, 84, 91, 110, 122.
  See also civil unions
school prayer, 21, 64, 84
Schundler, Bret, 88
Schwerner, Michael, 37
searching students, 77–78
secret detainees, 101–106
segregation
  core of racial, 11
  in Levittown, 5–8
Seldin, Abbe, 48, 51–52, 51*ph*
Selective Service System, 2, 35, 36

separation of church and state, 65, 88
sex discrimination cases, 41–43,
    45–46, 50, 73. *See also* gender
    equality cases
sex offenders, 114–115
sexual revolution, 32
Shepard, Matthew, 83
Sheppard, Annamay, 34, 47, 48,
    48*ph*, 52
shopping malls, protesting at, 82–83
Sills, Arthur, 39
Smith, John, 30
social media, 121–122
Social Security Administration, 2,
    41–43, 45–46
Socialist Labor Party (NYC), 60
Socialist Workers Party, 60
South Jersey, 21, 57, 68, 84
Southern California ACLU, 37
Spaulding Frazer of Newark
    (attorneys), 14
"Special Registration" program, 105
Spina, Dominick, 26
Spock, Benjamin, 33, 35
The Star-Ledger of Newark, 58
State Police, New Jersey
    harassment of long-haired men,
        47–49, 79–80
    during 1967 Newark rebellion, 26
    profiling drivers. *See also* racial
        profiling, 79–80, 97–98, 107,
        113–114
"Statewide Crisis in Policing"
    (report), 117
Stavis, Morton, 30
Steinem, Gloria, 42
Stewart, Potter, 45
Stockton State College (NJ), 115
Students for a Democratic Society, 22
Sunder, Madhavi, 74, 74*ph*

Sussex County, 11
Swedesboro (NJ), 57

T

Tan, Terry, 112, 112*ph*
Taub, Nadine, 47, 67–68, 75
Teaneck High School (NJ), 51
Thomas, Norman, 14
Thompson, Anne E., 96
Tiger Inn Club, 73, 75
transgender rights, 110, 113
Trenton, 5, 37, 67
Trenton Board of Education, 21
Trenton State Prison, 54, 56
Tropic of Cancer (Miller), 2
Truman, Harry S., 7
Twin Rivers Homeowners'
    Association, 109

U

U. S. Occupational Safety and
    Health Administration, 58
Union City (NJ), 12
Union County, 116–117
University of Wyoming, 83
unreasonable search and seizure, 43,
    55, 61, 77–78
Urban League, 30
Urban Legal Clinic, 46–47
urine testing, 78
U.S. Army
    desegregation of, 7
    investigation of installation by
        McCarthy, 18–19
    surveillance program of
        activists, 40
U.S. Immigration and
    Naturalization Service, 101

USA Patriot Act, 101

V

Verniero, Peter, 96, 98
Vietnam War, 2, 32, 35, 121

W

Wagner Act af 1935, 13–14
Waldman, Herbert, 36
Walker, Samuel, 19
Warren County (NJ), 89
Washington, 22
Washington Borough, 89
Watts riot (CA), 37
Weather Underground, 27
Weinberger v. Wisenfeld, 45
Weinglass, Leonard, 27
Wenk, Marsha, 84, 84*ph*, 90
West Morris-Mendham High
    School, 59–60
West New York Police
    Department, 93
Westbrooks, Dennis, 31
Westville (NJ), 79
Whitman, Christine Todd, 83, 85,
    95–98
Wiesenfeld, Jason, 42, 45, 46
Wiesenfeld, Paula, 42–43
Wiesenfeld, Stephen, 2, 41–43,
    41*ph*, 45–46
Wilentz, Robert N., 85–86, 86
Williams, Carl, 98
Willingboro (NJ), 5–7, 33
Wolfe, Tom, 47, 85
Women's Organization for the
    Return of Law and Decency, 24
women's rights, 50, 67–68, 90, 110

Women's Rights Litigation Clinic,
    47, 75
Women's Rights Project, 43, 50,
    67, 68
Woodbridge (NJ), 53
Woodstown High School, 71
World Trade Center (NYC)
    attack on, 99–100
    detentions after attack on,
    101–106
World War II (WWII), U.S. enters,
    14–15
Wynn, Brendan, 32
Wynn v. Byrne, 32, 33
Wysoker, Jack, 33, 33*ph*

Y

YWCA v. Kugler, 50

Z

Zimmerman, Perry, 19